THROUGH THE ARCH

E.S.T. 75 1938
YEARS
THE UNIVERSITY OF GEORGIA PRESS 2013

Through the Arch

An Illustrated Guide to the University of Georgia Campus

Larry B. Dendy   FOREWORD BY F. N. BONEY

The University of Georgia Press   ATHENS & LONDON

© 2013 by the University of Georgia Press
Athens, Georgia 30602
www.ugapress.org
All rights reserved

Designed by Erin Kirk New
Set in ITC Legacy
Manufactured by Versa Press using 100% PCW,
Processed Chlorine Free, acid-free, Forest Stewardship
Council-certified Anthem Matte paper as text stock

The paper in this book meets the guidelines for
permanence and durability of the Committee on
Production Guidelines for Book Longevity of the
Council on Library Resources.

Printed in the United States of America
17 16 15 14 13 P 5 4 3 2 1

Library of Congress Cataloging-in-Publication Data

Dendy, Larry B., 1943–
  Through the arch : an illustrated guide to the University of
Georgia campus / Larry Dendy.
     pages cm.
  Includes index.
   ISBN-13: 978-0-8203-4248-1 (pbk. : alk. paper)
   ISBN-10: 0-8203-4248-3 (pbk. : alk. paper)
    1. University of Georgia—Guidebooks. 2. University of Georgia—
Buildings—Guidebooks. 3. Athens (Ga.)—Buildings, structures, etc.—
Guidebooks. I. Title.
   LD1984.D46 2013
   378.00958'18—dc23   2013003512

British Library Cataloging-in-Publication Data available

This book is supported in part by the President's Venture Fund through the generous gifts of the University of Georgia Partners and other donors, as well as by the Frances Wood Wilson Foundation and the Willson Center for Humanities and Arts.

Willson Center
for humanities
& arts

CONTENTS

FOREWORD

CHARTERED IN 1785 and first holding classes in 1801, the University of Georgia has been around for a long time by U.S. standards. Though chartered as the nation's first public institution of higher education, for a century the school operated instead as a small, all-white, all-male, church-related, private liberal arts college that resembled its nearby rivals, Mercer, Emory, and Oglethorpe. With only one hundred students at the beginning of the Civil War in 1861 and barely three hundred at the end of that century forty years later, it was one of the nation's handful of real colleges, educating a very small percentage of the nation's population, mostly a privileged minority of white males. One of the very few colleges for women, Georgia Female College (now Wesleyan College in Macon), was founded by a UGA graduate, who modeled it after his alma mater.

Around 1900, UGA finally began to evolve into a modern state university that served all Georgians—or at least the white majority. The admission of women in 1918 pushed enrollment to more than a thousand, though the student body remained all-white for over four more decades. The emergence of a true federal land-grant college on the new South Campus pleased the agrarian masses, and the development of big-time football and other athletics further enhanced the popularity of a school in transition.

Slow but steady growth continued until December 7, 1941, when the Japanese attack on Pearl Harbor hurled the nation into World War II. When the men marched off to war, women temporarily became the majority of students. During the war, a six-thousand-man naval preflight program rotated young officers through a three-month training program, taking over many of the North and South Campus buildings and facilities and adding some new ones. The war effort revitalized the national economy. When veterans returned en masse in 1945, they flooded into the nation's colleges and universities under the auspices of the new GI Bill of Rights. Higher education boomed as never before.

Georgia (the state and the university) took full advantage of these trends. UGA's postwar enrollment approached eight thousand, trended down a little as the vets graduated, and then grew to well over eight thousand by 1961. But Georgia (the state and the university) still faced a major hurdle: segregation. That system, which placed the needs of whites before those of blacks, came under increasing fire from the public and the courts. The Supreme Court decision in 1954 abolishing legally mandated segregation in public education was resisted by all the southern states, but open defiance soon began to crumble. The first major breach in the wall of separation in Georgia occurred at UGA in January 1961, when the first two black undergraduates were admitted. After a few bumps and starts, Georgia (the state and the university) surged into the mainstream of U.S. life.

During the following half century, enrollment soared to thirty-five thousand, with the faculty likewise growing in quantity and quality. New buildings and sites of every size and function mushroomed, and in the 1990s the brand-new East Campus emerged. Outreach programs proliferated, and the school's national and international reputation rose rapidly. Now, the old North Campus, the newer South Campus, and the very new East Campus, as well as a recently designated Central Campus (squeezed onto recent campus maps between the north and south areas) all merge to reveal a proud school reaching for the stars.

As a graduate of little Hampden-Sydney College, I could relate well to what UGA must have been like in the nineteenth century, and graduate degrees from the University of Virginia in the early 1960s made me appreciate the boom times after World War II. Three books and dozens of articles and hundreds of lectures on UGA and twenty-eight years teaching in LeConte Hall and another seventeen years on campus in retirement (sort of) have given me some expertise on the subject. Remember the old chestnut "In the land of the blind, the one-eyed man is king." Well, most students and alumni are not blind to UGA, and I have a little better than a one-eyed perspective, but still the whole story is long and complex and can leave even experts a little dizzy.

This new volume by Larry Dendy is a fine addition to the literature on UGA—and a good remedy for partial dizziness. Starting with a succinct historical overview and including a summary of many campus traditions and a bibliography, and reinforced with many illustrations, it takes the reader-walker on a lengthy, detailed, precise grand tour of the campus or campuses and clearly describes the great changes that have occurred over the years. Even the old North Campus buildings and sites have undergone many changes. The first permanent building, Old College, served as a dormitory, classroom, and chow hall, and then hosted the navy in World War II, and now houses administrative offices, as do many of the other original buildings. Herty Field was the first rough athletic field and then served as an asphalt-paved parking lot and now has emerged as a beautiful park. The newer South Campus has evolved mainly from a thinly settled agricultural-education area into a densely packed bastion of science and technology; it is also the impressive home base of a high-powered athletic program. The much newer East Campus is even more marked by modern facilities. The newly designated Central Campus has many state-of-the-art student activity structures but also some older ones, such as Sanford Stadium, which keeps expanding, and Memorial Hall, which began as an athletic and recreational center and over the years has housed student and faculty dining halls, a bookstore, a library, a student radio station, athletic and administrative offices, a residence for international students, and a World War II home for the navy, which added a large annex. It is probably the champion of change as well as the most confusing labyrinth for the newcomer to navigate.

In recent times, huge influxes of private and governmental funds, including the highly successful HOPE scholarship program, have helped transform the whole university, fueling the massive building program but also funding a new sustainability movement that manages and protects the natural environment, as well as simple beautification projects in areas long neglected. In every way the old school is on the march, and this new volume is an excellent road map to the past, the present, and even the future.

Larry Dendy is an excellent guide to this increasingly complex story. A native of Atlanta, he graduated from the university in 1965, having majored in journalism and serving as an editor of the *Red and Black*. After a stint in the Peace Corps in India, work as a reporter at the *Columbus (Ga.) Ledger* and the *Atlanta Journal*, and work as a newspaper reporter and editor in Winston-Salem, North Carolina, and Tifton, Georgia, he "came home to momma" and served in the Office of Public Affairs for thirty-seven years as a writer, editor, news director, and special projects manager until he retired (sort of) in 2008 as assistant to the vice president for public affairs. He is credentialed to the hilt, and he has fulfilled that promise with this splendid addition to the literature on this fine old school, which has an even finer future.

F. N. BONEY

PREFACE

DURING THIRTY-SEVEN YEARS spent working in the University of Georgia public affairs office, I absorbed a great deal of knowledge about the campus and its history, traditions, and growth. I wrote thousands of news stories, magazine articles, speeches, reports, scripts, presentations, and other documents dealing with programs, people, policies, and activities at UGA. That background and familiarity with the university enabled me to write this book, which presents UGA in a novel way—by surveying the history, appearance, and use of more than 140 of its most important buildings, structures, and spaces.

In many ways, these facilities are the public face of the university, yet they receive little attention in most publications about UGA. Many structures and spaces are well over one hundred years old or are nearing the century mark, and so examining them can provide a useful historical context for the contemporary university. But this book is not meant to be a history of UGA. That history is well documented in the fine scholarly works of Robert Brooks, Thomas Dyer, and J. Thomas Bowen and in Nash Boney's popular pictorial history. Those authors do an excellent job of examining in depth the events, economic and political forces, personalities, and societal influences that have shaped the university over more than two centuries.

This book has a different purpose. It is intended to showcase and celebrate the beauty, historical significance, and academic strength of one of the leading public universities in the United States. In addition, the focus on buildings and spaces makes this book a convenient, informative guide to navigating the campus and enjoying its unique features.

The book deals solely with the university's Athens campus and major facilities in Clarke and nearby counties. But it should be noted that as Georgia's flagship land-grant university, UGA has a statewide presence and impact. There are UGA facilities or personnel in almost every county in Georgia, including extended campuses in Griffin, Tifton, and Gwinnett County, where students earn academic credit toward UGA degrees. The university's vast public service and outreach programs assist communities and citizens throughout the state, and research by university scientists and scholars benefits agriculture, forestry, business, education, and other sectors of Georgia's economy. While this book spotlights only the main Athens campus, in a larger sense UGA's campus is the entire state of Georgia.

Writing a book that describes the university's physical appearance and characteristics has an inherent problem: inevitably, those features will change. UGA is a dynamic, ever-growing, ever-evolving institution, and what was accurate at the time of publication may not be accurate a few years later. New buildings will be erected; existing buildings will be revamped or razed; occupants or usages of buildings will change. Enhancements will be added to the campus to accommodate technological and environmental advances, and outdated infrastructure will be removed. Such changes are desirable as the university grows and improves to meet the evolving needs of students, faculty, and staff. But readers should remember that a campus is a moving target, and this book can capture only a snapshot from the vantage point of one particular moment in time.

I want to acknowledge some people who helped make the book possible. I want to thank Nancy Grayson, former associate director of the University of Georgia Press, and former Press staff members Judy Purdy and Lane Stewart for their confidence in asking me to undertake this project. I appreciate Tom Jackson, UGA's vice president for public affairs, for providing me with work space, a computer, and access to files and documents in the Hodgson Oil Building. Thanks to my former public affairs workmates for their friendship and help, especially Alison Huff, publications director in the office and my technology guru, whose patience, assurance, and good sense several times prevented me from chucking my computer out the window and leaping out after it. Thanks also to Dot Paul in the public affairs photography department for searching out and supplying the beautiful photographs in the book, and to Greg Gotsch in the University Architect's office for providing the helpful maps. Many people answered my questions, provided facts and data, and guided me to other sources of information. I particularly want to acknowledge Steven Brown of the UGA libraries, whose encyclopedic knowledge of UGA was invaluable in supplying information I couldn't find elsewhere and in choosing the historical photographs for the book, and Scott Messer in the University Architect's office, who patiently allowed me to invade his office to peruse his files on buildings.

I also want to thank Regan Huff, my editor at the Press, for her patience in shepherding me through the perplexities of book publishing, and Catherine Jean (C. J.) Bartunek for her diligent but amiable help in gathering and organizing the material in the book. I am grateful to Nash Boney for writing the foreword to the book, and I am deeply indebted to Nash, Tom Dyer, Tom Bowen, and Danny Sniff for their meticulous scholarship, which I relied on so heavily. Finally, I want to thank family members and friends who uplifted me with their confidence and encouragement, especially my wife, Gail, who tolerated my absences, put up with my grumpiness, gave me sound advice and helpful criticism, and lovingly supported and sustained me through this adventure.

LARRY DENDY

THROUGH THE ARCH

By the Representatives of the Free...

And by the Authority of the...

... Therefore ...

Enacted Ordained and Declared. —

the Board of Visitors ...

academies ...

... Trustees of the University, Geor...

... Senatus Academicus ...

Provided ...

CHAPTER 1

Brief History

"AS IT IS THE DISTINGUISHING HAPPINESS of free governments that civil Order should be the Result of choice and not necessity, and the common wishes of the People become the Laws of the Land, their public prosperity and even existence very much depends upon suitably forming the minds and morals of their Citizens."

Those words, penned in the late eighteenth century by Abraham Baldwin, set the stage for one of the most transformative innovations in the history of the United States. The words are the first sentence of the University of Georgia Charter—the document that laid the foundation for the great U.S. system of public higher education.

The American Revolution had just ended and the U.S. Constitution had not yet been adopted when Baldwin arrived in Georgia in 1783 from his native Connecticut. The young Yale-educated minister and lawyer quickly made his presence known in the largely unsettled frontier of the former thirteen colony. Intelligent, articulate, and ambitious, he won election to the General Assembly in 1784 and soon was caught up in an enterprise that would earn him a place in history.

Higher education in the young United States was confined to a dozen small colleges, some church affiliated, located mainly in the Northeast, that enrolled students from wealthy, influential families. For most ordinary citizens, college was out of reach, and that was certainly true in Georgia. Largely wilderness, populated mainly by Native Americans, struggling farmers, and small merchants, the state in fact had no colleges and only a few private academies in small towns. State leaders understood that an educated population would be necessary if the state were to grow, but they also knew citizens did not have resources to support a college. Higher education would be possible only with state backing.

In February 1784, the General Assembly earmarked forty thousand acres of land to be sold to fund "a college or seminary of learning." Abraham

The Georgia General Assembly adopted Abraham Baldwin's charter for the University of Georgia on January 27, 1785. The action created the first college in America established by a state government, and laid the groundwork for the eventual emergence of some seventeen hundred state colleges and universities—the bedrock of America's system of public higher education.

Baldwin—one of the best-educated legislators—was appointed to a legislative committee to begin organizing the college and was given the task of writing a charter.

Inspired by the nation's recent triumph for freedom and democracy, Baldwin infused his charter with populist concepts that were unorthodox at the time: a popular government can succeed only if its citizens are educated; all citizens—not just the wealthy and privileged—have a right to education, and none should be excluded because of religious affiliation; and—perhaps most crucially—government is obligated to make education available to citizens. A college founded on these principles, the charter said, would "form the youth, the rising hope of our land, to render the like glorious and essential services to our country."

The General Assembly adopted Baldwin's charter on January 27, 1785. The action created the first college in the United States established by a state government and laid the groundwork for the eventual emergence of some seventeen hundred state colleges and universities—the bedrock of the U.S. system of public higher education.

Baldwin was appointed president of the new university and chair of a board of trustees assigned to get the school started. The trustees, part of a larger oversight group called the Senatus Academicus, met a few times, but more pressing problems diverted the attention of state leaders, and for sixteen years the university existed only on paper. Finally, near the end of the eighteenth century, interest in the university was revived, and the Senatus Academicus formed a five-man delegation to find a site for the school. The committee included Baldwin, who had been elected to the U.S. Senate but continued to hold the title of president; John Milledge, a Revolutionary War veteran who would become the next governor of Georgia; and William Few, who—along with Baldwin—had signed the U.S. Constitution on behalf of Georgia.

In the spring of 1801, the committee journeyed deep into the rugged interior of the state. Near the edge of Indian territory, in what was then Jackson County, the group came upon a small settlement on the Oconee River. A mill owner, Daniel Easley, showed the group a spot on a wooded hill above the west side of the river shoals. The site seemed ideal: a pristine forest with clear streams, unlikely to harbor diseases, secluded from the temptations of town life that might distract young men from scholarly pursuits. Though the state owned five thousand acres nearby from the original forty-thousand-acre grant, the committee decided this was where the University of Georgia should be.

Milledge paid Easley $4,000 for 633 acres and immediately gave the land to the Senatus Academicus. Baldwin resigned as president and was succeeded by Josiah Meigs, a Yale mathematics and philosophy teacher whom Baldwin had taught at Yale. Meigs arrived in the summer of 1801 and began clearing an opening in the forest for a small log cabin to serve as a classroom. He also began recruiting students from academies, and in September 1801 he taught the first class to a group of about thirty young men. The University of Georgia had at last begun.

The young school offered a classical liberal arts curriculum of Latin, Greek, mathematics, rhetoric, and natural history, all taught initially by Meigs. Some of the boys who enrolled were only thirteen or fourteen years old and unprepared for advanced academic work, so Meigs erected a wooden building to serve as a grammar school. The university students formed a debating group, the Demosthenian Literary Society, in 1803, and the next year the first commencement ceremony was held, with diplomas presented to nine graduates.

The trustees sold off some land to raise money to construct a permanent brick building. By the time the structure was completed in 1806, the land was supporting a community of homes and shops that was incorporated as Athens. The building, known at first as Franklin College (in honor of Benjamin Franklin) and later as Old College, was for fifteen years the dormitory, dining hall, and classroom facility for university students.

The state's initial land endowment failed to produce much income, and with meager support from the financially strapped legislature and little interest from citizens, the young university was soon in serious financial trouble. Meigs resigned in frustration in 1810, and the school struggled under the next two presidents, briefly ceasing operations twice. By 1819 the university had dwindled to seven students, three teachers, and one academic building. It survived mainly through the determined efforts of the fifth president, Moses Waddel, who served from 1819 to 1829, and his successor, Alonzo Church (1829–59). Stern Presbyterian ministers and academic traditionalists, Waddel and Church labored relentlessly to recruit students, stabilize finances, add faculty members, and erect buildings, including the landmark New College (1823) and Chapel (1832).

In 1834, Augustin S. Clayton, a member of the first graduating class, founded the University Alumni Society. In 1854, William Terrell, a wealthy Georgia planter, donated $20,000 to create the first endowed faculty position, a chair in agriculture; that endowment laid the groundwork for UGA's future leadership in agricultural education and outreach.

Signers of Constitution

Abraham Baldwin, who wrote UGA's charter, and William Few, an early member of the university's board of trustees, signed the U.S. Constitution in 1787 on behalf of Georgia.

By 1859, when the school had more than one hundred students and eight faculty members, university trustees felt confident enough to adopt a reorganization plan for a modernized academic structure that would be more like a true university. In addition to the Franklin College of Arts and Sciences, the plan called for schools of law, agriculture, engineering, and commerce, and for postgraduate degrees in medicine and divinity. The law school was started in 1859, just as Church retired, leaving the plan in the hands of his successor, Andrew Lipscomb, who took office in 1860 with the new title of chancellor. A former Methodist minister who never attended college, Lipscomb was nevertheless a respected educator who had been president of a girls' college in Alabama. Unfortunately, he arrived at UGA on the brink of the Civil War, which derailed much of the ambitious reorganization plan, including the start-up of the other schools.

More than half the students, along with several faculty members, joined the Confederate army when the war started in 1861, and more left as the fighting continued. In the fall of 1863, with the campus nearly vacant, Lipscomb closed the university. It did not reopen until January 1866.

Except for a small skirmish near Watkinsville, no major Civil War battles were fought near Athens, and the university was not seriously harmed, though some buildings were damaged by Union soldiers who briefly encamped in Athens after the war. But UGA did not escape the war's human toll: some 100 students, teachers, and alumni died and many more suffered injuries.

Ironically, war's end brought UGA a period of brief prosperity as returning veterans enrolled under a state plan that paid them $300 for each year they agreed to stay in Georgia and teach after graduating. Enrollment topped three hundred—the highest ever—but dropped as the veterans departed, leaving the university again in severe financial straits.

Much-needed assistance came in 1872 with the university's designation as a land-grant college under the Morrill Act, which Congress had passed in 1862 to support schools that taught "agriculture and mechanic arts." The state of Georgia's federal allotment of $243,000 was turned over to the university, which invested the funds and used the resulting annual income of about $16,000 to establish the Georgia State College of Agriculture and Mechanic Arts (A&M). Though technically separate and independent from the university, the A&M college became a prime source of income as much of its federal funding was absorbed into the university's budget, probably staving off bankruptcy during the lean Reconstruction years. In the early twentieth century, under the forceful leadership of President Andrew Soule, the A&M college significantly expanded and strengthened agricultural education on campus and began to extend the university's reach by channeling academic resources and expertise to help citizens around the state. That early initiative helped pave the way for the university's vast program of public service and outreach.

Land-grant colleges were required to offer military training, which UGA began in the 1870s. The first social fraternity, Sigma Alpha Epsilon, was established in 1866 and was soon followed by seven more Greek organizations.

In 1886, the fraternities started the university yearbook, the *Pandora*, and in 1893 the Demosthenian and Phi Kappa literary societies cooperated to publish a student newspaper, the *Red and Black*. Baseball became the university's first intercollegiate sport when a team was formed in 1886, followed in 1892 by a football team organized and coached by Charles Herty. Baseball and football games were played on a scrabbly field just west of the campus now known as Herty Field.

Since its beginning, the university essentially had been a small, cloistered liberal arts college, led mostly by Protestant ministers and attended mainly by the white male children of middle- and upper-class Georgia families. That began to change in 1899 with the appointment of Walter B. Hill as chancellor. Hill, who had earned a bachelor's degree from the university in 1870 and master's and law degrees in 1871, was the first alumnus and only the second native Georgian (and second non-minister) to lead the institution. Energetic, innovative, and visionary, he was the first of a new generation of progressive, enlightened leaders who envisioned a bolder, more vigorous university, one that would serve all Georgia citizens.

Herty Field

Hill died of pneumonia after only six years, but his tenure was marked by important advances, including enrollment growth, curriculum expansion, and increased state funding (the General Assembly passed a bill in 1900 that provided an annual appropriation to UGA, and income topped $100,000 for the first time in 1902). In addition, Hill started a summer school to train teachers and initiated steps to modernize and strengthen agricultural education through the A&M college. He was succeeded in 1906 by another alumnus, David C. Barrow, a native Athenian and 1874 graduate, who served until 1925 and carried forward many of Hill's initiatives. Under Hill, Barrow, and their successors Charles Snelling (1926–32), Steadman Sanford (1932–35), and Harmon Caldwell (1935–48), UGA grew significantly and took on the character of a true university.

Sea Grant College

In addition to its status as a land-grant institution, UGA has been designated a Sea Grant College by the National Oceanic and Atmospheric Administration in recognition of its excellence in marine research, education, and advisory services.

An aerial view of Ag Hill and Conner Hall, 1927

Electricity, municipal water lines, and steam heat came to the campus in the early twentieth century, making buildings more comfortable and reducing fire hazards. Better funding from the state, along with increased private support, most notably from the philanthropist George Foster Peabody, sparked dramatic growth in academic offerings and expansion of the campus. The School of Pharmacy was established in 1903, and in 1906 the General Assembly created a College of Agriculture, which included the A&M college and a small college of science and engineering. The School of Forestry began in 1906 also, followed by the School of Education (1908), Graduate School (1910), School of Commerce (1912), and School of Journalism (1915). The first chapter of the Phi Beta Kappa scholastic honor society in Georgia was established at UGA in 1914.

The opening of Conner Hall in 1908 on a high hill south of the original North Campus extended the campus into a largely undeveloped area that quickly became South Campus. The vanguard for an invigorated agricultural program, Conner Hall was followed by many other agricultural buildings in an area that became known as "Ag Hill."

In 1891, the General Assembly started a State Normal School a few miles west of campus to train young men and women to be schoolteachers. Though the university admitted only males as regular students, it began allowing female graduates of the Normal School, which technically was part of the university, to enroll in summer school classes for postgraduate work. After the Graduate School was started, female teachers from around the state were admitted to summer school for graduate work, and some female Normal School students were quietly allowed to attend regular classes. By 1914, Mary D. Lyndon had accumulated enough credits to qualify for a master's degree in education; she became the first woman to receive a UGA degree. Finally, in 1918, after years of urging by the Daughters of the American Revolution and United Daughters of the Confederacy, UGA became one of the last universities in the South to admit women as regular students.

Mary Creswell

The first female students enrolled at the junior and senior level in a division of home economics in the College of Agriculture and Mechanic Arts. In 1919, Mary E. Creswell received a bachelor's degree in home economics, becoming the first woman to earn an undergraduate degree. Soule Hall, the first dormitory for women, opened in 1920, and the next year women were admitted at the freshman and sophomore level. The admission of women helped spike enrollment, which topped 1,000 for the first time in 1919 and reached 1,691 in 1928, when a women's physical education building opened.

Coeds, 1924

UGA Presidents and Chancellors

Twenty-two men have served as president or chancellor of the University of Georgia. They are:

Abraham Baldwin (1785–1801)
Josiah Meigs (1801–10)
John Brown (1811–16)
Robert Finley (1817)
Moses Waddel (1819–29)
Alonzo Church (1829–59)
Andrew Lipscomb (1860–74)
Henry Tucker (1874–78)
Patrick Mell (1878–88)
William Boggs (1889–99)
Walter Hill (1899–1905)
David Barrow (1906–25)
Charles Snelling (1926–32)
Steadman Sanford (1932–35)
Harmon Caldwell (1935–48)
Jonathan Rogers (1949–50)
Omer Clyde (O. C.) Aderhold (1950–67)
Fred Davison (1967–86)
Henry Stanford (1986–87)
Charles Knapp (1987–97)
Michael Adams (1997–2013)
Jere Morehead (2013–   )

The title of the university's leader was changed from president to chancellor as part of a reorganization plan in 1859. The title was changed back to president in 1932 when the University System of Georgia was created and its top official was given the title of chancellor. Those who held the title of chancellor at UGA were Andrew Lipscomb, Henry Tucker, Patrick Mell, William Boggs, Walter Hill, David Barrow and Charles Snelling.

The UGA presidents and chancellors who served the longest are Alonzo Church (thirty years), David Barrow (nineteen years), Fred Davison (nineteen years), O. C. Aderhold (seventeen years), Abraham Baldwin (sixteen years), and Michael Adams (sixteen years). Robert Finley, who died of typhus several months after taking office, had the shortest term. Patrick Mell died in the tenth year of his tenure, and Walter Hill died after six years in office.

UGA participated in a World War I government program to train students for army commissions, and after the war several hundred veterans enrolled in a government program designed to help educate veterans. More than sixteen hundred men who had been university students or alumni fought in the war, and forty-seven alumni were killed. Their names are inscribed in the rotunda of Memorial Hall, which was called War Memorial Hall when it opened in 1925. The building was completed with proceeds from the War Memorial Fund campaign organized after the war by the Alumni Society.

With the admission of women and the expansion of the curriculum afforded by the new schools, enrollment had risen to two thousand by 1932. The men's athletic program grew to include basketball, golf, boxing, lacrosse, and tennis. But football was the king of sports on campus, and in 1929 the gridiron Bulldogs moved to Sanford Stadium, a spacious arena that seated thirty thousand and had a unique feature—a row of small hedges encircling the playing field. In the inaugural game, played October 12, 1929, Georgia defeated Yale 15–0.

The creation of the University System of Georgia in 1932 consolidated UGA and the state's other public colleges—which had been run by independent boards of trustees—under the centralized administrative control of a board of regents. Several university branch campuses became separate institutions, each with its own president. On the Athens campus, the State College of Agriculture and Mechanic Arts was merged into the College of Agriculture. The State Normal School, which had been renamed the State Teachers College, was absorbed by the School of Education, and its campus became the UGA "Coordinate Campus," the home of freshman and sophomore women. All UGA engineering programs except agricultural engineering were transferred to Georgia Tech, which sent its commerce program to UGA.

The title of the head of the university had been changed from president to chancellor when Andrew Lipscomb took the position in 1860. But the top official of the new university system was given the title of chancellor, so the university had to revert back to the title of president for its leader. Charles Snelling, who was UGA chancellor when the university system was created, was tapped to be its first chancellor. Steadman Sanford was named his successor as university president in 1932, and three years later Sanford was appointed to succeed Snelling as system chancellor. His successor as president, Harmon Caldwell, then followed Sanford as chancellor in 1948.

Despite the economic challenges of the Depression, the university continued to advance. The School of Home Economics was established in 1933, incorporating courses that had been taught in the agriculture and education schools. With adoption of the academic quarter system, a set of required core courses for freshmen and sophomores was instituted. With tuition relatively low (forty dollars each quarter) and jobs scarce, students flooded the university, sending enrollment soaring above three thousand for the first time in 1937 and to almost four thousand by 1941.

Even as it caused hardships for the university, the Depression, ironically, helped spark a period of unprecedented growth. Through the Public Works Administration, created as part of President Franklin D. Roosevelt's New Deal, UGA received almost $2 million, which was supplemented by another $1 million from the state legislature. The university used the money between 1936 and the early 1940s for a building blitz that included five new or expanded residence halls, eight classroom buildings, a dining hall, a nursery school, four "home management laboratories," and other structures for teaching and agricultural use. Rudolph Driftmier, an engineering professor, and Roy Hitchcock, an architect, designed many of the buildings in a neoclassical style, thereby saving the university expensive architectural fees and creating a distinctive similarity in the appearance of buildings. PWA funds were used also to renovate and upgrade existing buildings, pave campus roads and sidewalks, and install landscaping.

In 1941, UGA and nine other schools in the University System of Georgia were stripped of accreditation by the Southern Association of Colleges and Secondary Schools after Governor Eugene Talmadge interfered with decisions of the board of regents. The controversy arose when Talmadge used his regent-appointing power as a way to force the board to oust the dean of UGA's College of Education, Walter Cocking, on charges he favored racial integration. The loss of accreditation became a major issue in the 1942 gubernatorial election, in which Talmadge sought reelection. He was soundly defeated by Georgia attorney general Ellis Arnall, who promised to make the board of regents independent of political interference. In one of his first acts as governor, Arnall pushed through the legislature a constitutional amendment that restructured the board and removed the governor as an ex officio member—a move that quickly led to restoration of accreditation for UGA and the other schools.

Leadership for Georgia

Twenty-five governors of Georgia have been UGA graduates, as have many of the state's U.S. senators and congressmen. Scores of UGA graduates have served in the Georgia General Assembly and held offices in state government. Many have served as justices in federal courts, the Georgia Supreme Court, the Georgia Court of Appeals, and in numerous other judicial posts.

Navy preflight cadets

The university was growing and in relatively stable financial condition when the United States entered World War II. Enrollment fell as male students, teachers, and staff members enlisted; for the first time, women outnumbered men on campus. But the absence of students became less noticeable once the army and navy began operating training programs at UGA. The navy's preflight training school was the largest, bringing more than twenty thousand young men to campus in three-month cycles over a three-year period. To accommodate the cadets, the navy commandeered many campus buildings and extensively reconfigured the interiors of some of the university's oldest structures. The navy enlarged some buildings and erected several new ones, most of which no longer exist. Construction costs for the navy's stay on campus totaled about $550,000, of which the navy paid $318,671.

About two hundred university alumni and students died in World War II. As in the aftermath of previous wars, enrollment surged with the return of veterans, reaching nearly eight thousand by 1948. To house the veterans, many of whom were married with children, the university created a village of trailers and makeshift structures known as "prefabs" on South Campus. As the veterans graduated, enrollment dropped to around fifty-five hundred and did not reach eight thousand again for more than a decade.

In 1945, the New York art collector Alfred Holbrook gave UGA one hundred paintings to create the Georgia Museum of Art. Two years later, a quarterly literary journal, the *Georgia Review*, began publication. The art museum, the *Review*, and the University of Georgia Press, organized in 1938, along with strong academic programs in music and art, helped make UGA a cornerstone of literary and fine arts achievement in Georgia. The School of Veterinary Medicine was reestablished in 1946 after having been discontinued thirteen years earlier when the veterinary program was part of the agricultural college. All the expansive agricultural programs, including the College of Agriculture, agricultural experiment stations, and the Cooperative Extension Service, were combined under one dean.

The appointment of Omer Clyde (O. C.) Aderhold as president in 1950 opened another era of growth and progress. Aderhold, who served until 1967, and his successors, Fred Davison (1967–86), Charles Knapp (1987–97), and Michael F. Adams (1997–2013), advanced the university from a small, relatively obscure state school into a major regional, national, and international university that is widely respected for excellence and achievement in research, teaching, and public service.

Aderhold, who held bachelor's and master's degrees from UGA and was dean of the College of Education before becoming president, appointed the first vice presidents for research and public service, creating the model for the university's modern administrative structure. Aderhold emphasized graduate and professional studies, and the number of master's degrees awarded annually tripled during his tenure. Freshman and sophomore women, who had been living on the Coordinate Campus, returned to the main campus when the university sold the Coordinate Campus to the U.S. Navy as a training school for supply officers. The Ilah Dunlap Little Memorial Library (the "main library") opened in 1952, and the School of Social Work was started in 1964.

Like many major southern state universities, the University of Georgia had an unwritten but clearly understood policy of not admitting African American students. Those policies began to crumble when the Supreme Court in *Brown v. Board of Education* (1954) declared public schools segregated by law to be unconstitutional; the ensuing civil rights movement brought racial exclusion under attack at many schools, including UGA.

In the summer of 1959, Hamilton Holmes, the valedictorian of his class at Atlanta's all-black Turner High School, and Charlayne Hunter, the editor of the school's newspaper, filed applications to enter UGA. Their requests were denied (allegedly because of a lack of dormitory space). Holmes enrolled at Morehouse College, and Hunter at Wayne State University. But their lawyers continued to fight for their admission to UGA, finally taking the case to U.S. district court. On January 6, 1961, Judge W. A. Bootle ended 160 years of segregation at UGA by ordering the university to allow Holmes and Hunter to transfer. Three days later, they walked through the Arch and into Academic Building, where they completed registration for winter quarter classes.

The graduation of Charlayne Hunter and Hamilton Holmes

Hunter was assigned a private suite on the ground floor of Myers Hall, while Holmes opted to live in a private home off campus. Their first two days on campus were tense but uneventful. But on the night of January 11, following the Georgia basketball team's close loss to rival Georgia Tech, a crowd of several hundred, including some nonstudents, converged on Myers Hall. Yelling epithets and threats, the demonstrators started fires and shattered windows of Hunter's rooms with rocks and bottles. University officials whisked Hunter from the building while Athens police and state patrol officers dispersed the mob with water hoses and tear gas. Hunter and Holmes were temporarily suspended "in the interest of public safety," and they spent the next few days in Atlanta while their attorneys worked through the courts to get them readmitted; 80 percent of university faculty members signed a petition calling for their reinstatement. When they returned on January 16, Hunter moved back into Myers Hall, and they resumed classes without further serious incident.

The following June, Mary Frances Early, a Turner High graduate who was studying for a master's degree at the University of Michigan, transferred to UGA to show support for Holmes and Hunter. Holmes, Hunter, and Early did not encounter further violence, and except for taunts and jeers they were largely ostracized by white students and made few friends. In 1962, Early received her master's degree in music, becoming the first African American to earn a diploma from UGA. Holmes, who was elected to Phi Beta Kappa, and Hunter graduated in the spring of 1963.

After returning to UGA to earn a specialist in education degree in 1967, Early taught music in Atlanta schools for thirty years. She was also a music professor at Morehouse College and Spelman College and served for eight years as chair of the music department at Clark College.

Holmes enrolled in Emory University's medical school—the first African American to do so—and graduated in 1967. He became a prominent Atlanta orthopedic surgeon, hospital administrator, and associate dean of the Emory medical school. He died unexpectedly in 1995.

Hunter, now Charlayne Hunter-Gault, wrote for the *New Yorker* magazine and the *New York Times* and was an anchor for *The MacNeil/Lehrer Report.* She became a correspondent for CNN and National Public Radio, winning several Peabody and Emmy Awards, and wrote two books, including an autobiographical account of her time at UGA.

For years after their graduation, Holmes, Hunter, and Early had no contact with the university and acknowledged feeling bitter about their treatment as students. But after the university reached out to them, each became a strong supporter. During its bicentennial celebration in 1985, the university presented Holmes and Hunter with the Bicentennial Medallion and created the Holmes-Hunter Lecture, which annually brings to campus a distinguished speaker to discuss a topic dealing with race relations or black history.

Holmes accepted an invitation to become the first African American trustee of the University of Georgia Foundation and was active in the Alumni Society. The College of Arts and Sciences created a professorship in his name, and he received the Blue Key Award and the Alumni Society's Distinguished Alumni Merit Award.

Hunter-Gault became the first African American to speak at a UGA commencement when she addressed the Class of 1988. She served on the advisory board of the Grady College of Journalism and Mass Communication and has returned to campus numerous times for speaking engagements and to meet with students.

Early was featured in a public television documentary about UGA's desegregation and spoke on campus a number of times, including delivering the commencement address for graduate students in 2007. As part of a ceremony in 2012 recognizing the fiftieth anniversary of her graduation, she donated her personal papers and memorabilia to the UGA library. The College of Education established a professorship in Early's name and presented her its Distinguished Alumni Award.

In 1992, Holmes and Hunter established a scholarship for African American students, and in 2001, as part of a celebration recognizing the fortieth anniversary of desegregation, the university named the Academic Building for Holmes and Hunter.

Mary Frances Early

As enrollment climbed in the early 1960s with the arrival of the first wave of post–World War II baby boomers, the university built a cluster of residence halls on the western edge of campus, including three high-rise dormitories, each housing nearly a thousand students. Responding to the nation's intensified focus on science and research following the Soviet Union's launch of the *Sputnik* satellite in 1957, the university constructed a six-building Science Center on the South Campus hill overlooking Sanford Stadium. When the pharmacy school moved from North Campus to its new South Campus facility in 1964, all science and agricultural units were located on South Campus, leaving North Campus the primary home of the humanities, arts, social sciences, and law.

Under Fred Davison, a UGA graduate and former dean of the College of Veterinary Medicine, the university advanced sharply in size, quality, and reputation. Davison's nineteen-year tenure centered on his unabashed goal of lifting the University of Georgia into the ranks of leading U.S. public universities. He succeeded by making scientific research a priority, especially biotechnology and its component disciplines, such as genetics, biochemistry, and plant cellular and molecular biology. The total research budget soared from $15.6 million to more than $90 million, the number of doctoral degrees awarded annually almost tripled, and more than seven hundred faculty members joined the university, including leading national scientists and scholars. In the 1970s, UGA was ranked in five national surveys as one of the top fifty research institutions in the United States.

The Miller Plant Sciences Building and the Ecology Building were among fifteen new buildings, valued at more than $150 million, constructed during the Davison administration. The university was designated a Sea Grant College for excellence in marine research and outreach, and the School of Environmental Design was established. As total enrollment climbed to an all-time high of twenty-five thousand, a long-awaited student center, named for the legendary dean of men William Tate, opened. In 1984, the university launched a fifteen-month celebration of its two-hundredth birthday, becoming the first public university in the country to observe a bicentennial. Part of the celebration included the first major fund-raising campaign in modern university history, which netted $93 million.

For all its successes, Davison's administration ended in unhappy controversy when Jan Kemp, a faculty member who helped tutor athletes, sued the university for failure to renew her contract. The court case, which drew national attention, raised allegations of lax scholastic standards and favoritism for athletes. Although it sullied the university's growing reputation for academic and scientific achievement, the case helped spawn a move toward important national reforms in academic requirements for collegiate athletes. When Kemp won a verdict of more than $1 million, Davison resigned.

Henry King Stanford, a former president of the University of Miami, came out of retirement to serve as interim president for a year. A sprightly septuagenarian with boundless energy and enthusiasm, Stanford made it his mission to rebuild the university's image and to rally public and political support for the school. His infectious goodwill and optimism lifted spirits and rejuvenated morale on the dejected campus, setting the stage for the arrival in 1987 of Charles Knapp.

Though descended from a line of distinguished educators, Knapp, an Iowa native who was executive vice president at Tulane University, was only the third permanent president in more than a century who was not born in Georgia or did not hold a UGA degree, and his selection was met with some skepticism. But his collegial, collaborative administrative style and bold vision for the university's future quieted doubts and earned him the respect and support of faculty, students, and alumni.

Knapp, too, emphasized research, and expenditures rose to $209 million, ranking UGA first in the nation for research spending among public institutions with neither medical nor engineering schools. The university became a founding partner of the Georgia Research Alliance, a collaboration between private corporations and the state's six research universities to foster technological innovation and economic growth. Knapp worked closely with Governor Zell Miller to create Georgia's HOPE Scholarship, and average Scholastic Achievement Test (SAT) scores of entering freshmen jumped ninety points, placing UGA among the top fifteen comprehensive public universities in the nation with the highest SAT scores.

After more than fifty years on the quarter system, the university adopted the semester academic calendar in 1998. A major fund-raising drive called the Third Century Campaign generated more than $151 million, making it the largest fund-raising effort in university history. In the summer of 1996, thousands of spectators flooded the campus as UGA hosted three events of the Atlanta Centennial Olympic Games—preliminary competitions in volleyball and rhythmic gymnastics, and the finals of women's soccer.

While he enjoyed success on many fronts, Knapp's defining legacy is probably his record of campus development, highlighted by the creation of East Campus. Implementing a then-novel financing approach of public-private partnerships, Knapp fulfilled a pledge to erect a new building for each of his ten years as president. Nearly $400 million in new construction,

The 1996 Olympics in Athens

renovations, and additions was completed, started, or planned, adding more than 1.2 million square feet to the campus space inventory.

Foremost in the flurry of construction was the transformation of acres of fields and woodlands on the southeastern edge of South Campus into the stunning East Campus. Opened in 1995, the new campus was anchored on the south by the mammoth Ramsey Student Physical Activities Center and on the north by the elegant Performing Arts Center, Georgia Museum of Art, and School of Music. The campus also included the university's first Visitors Center, a modern student health center, and a large animal-science complex that opened after Knapp left office.

Michael Adams, who succeeded Knapp in 1997, arrived, like his predecessor, with an ambitious agenda for growth and a promise to lead the university to higher levels of academic quality and national recognition. In a sixteen-year tenure that made him the fifth longest-serving active president in university history, Adams fulfilled that vow, and UGA today enjoys a position of unprecedented strength and stature.

Early on, Adams initiated the creation of a strategic plan for the twenty-first century. It committed the university to expand into new frontiers in teaching and learning, research, and global competitiveness. The plan identified one of those frontiers as medicine and health sciences. Building on existing programs in biotechnology, biological sciences, pharmacology, and related disciplines, the university, under the guidance of Provost Karen Holbrook and her successor, Arnett Mace, moved aggressively into the biomedical field, creating the Biomedical and Health Sciences Institute, the Cancer Center, the Center for Tropical and Emerging Global Diseases, and the Regenerative Bioscience Center. In 2005, the College of Public Health was formed to bring together programs in epidemiology, toxicology, biostatistics, environmental health, global health, and health promotion and behavior.

The medical initiative took a giant step forward when the university reacquired the former home of the Navy Supply Corps School in Athens and turned it into a medical education facility. The fifty-six-acre site, which previously was home of the State Normal School and served as the Coordinate Campus, had been a training school for navy supply officers since 1953. When it was closed in 2011 as part of a federal realignment of military bases, UGA and Georgia Health Sciences University in Augusta, which became Georgia Regents University in 2013, formed a partnership to use the site to train new physicians in basic science and clinical skills and then place them in residencies in area hospitals and clinics. Renamed the UGA Health Sciences Campus, the facility is also the home of the College of Public Health, where UGA and

GRU scientists collaborate on research to combat some of Georgia's most pressing medical problems.

The College of Public Health, founded in 2005, is one of five new schools or colleges started under Adams, each of which significantly expanded UGA's academic parameters. The College of Environment and Design and the School of Public and International Affairs, both created in 2001, were the first new schools at UGA in thirty-seven years. In 2007, the Eugene Odum School of Ecology became the world's first stand-alone school devoted to ecological research and teaching. The College of Engineering was formed in 2012 to foster interdisciplinary collaboration among more than one hundred faculty members involved in engineering-related teaching, research, and outreach. The college, which offers undergraduate and graduate degrees in many areas of engineering, is another way for UGA to meet Georgia's rapidly growing demand for technological expertise and innovation.

With enrollment topping 34,800 in 2009—due in part to new or expanded degree programs at UGA's extended campuses in Gwinnett County, Griffin, and Tifton—student quality peaked, with the highest freshman average SAT scores in history. Record numbers of students participated in study abroad, many at year-round residential programs in England, Italy, and Costa Rica. Private financial support reached record highs as annual giving exceeded $100 million for the first time. A capital campaign called Archway to Excellence, which was planned to last seven years, hit its $500 million goal sixteen months ahead of schedule and eventually topped $600 million. In 1999, former president Jimmy Carter and his wife, Rosalynn, received the inaugural Delta Prize for Global Understanding, an award established by UGA and Delta Air Lines to recognize people who help promote world peace. Other recipients have included Nelson Mandela, Mikhail Gorbachev, and Desmond Tutu.

Adams's decision in 2003 not to renew the contract of athletic director and former football coach Vince Dooley set off a chain of events that resulted in the university dropping its affiliation with the sixty-eight-year-old University of Georgia Foundation and creating a new organization, called the Arch Foundation, to receive and manage private donations. But the UGA Foundation continued to operate, managing assets of about $700 million, and the rift ended in 2011 when the two foundations agreed to merge under the name of the University of Georgia Foundation.

While almost every president in the century preceding Adams could claim credit for at least one or two new buildings, none of them could match Adams's record for campus development. In the first decade of his administration, more than $1 billion in new facilities and physical-plant

UGA Budget

Only about 31 percent of UGA's annual $1.35 billion budget is provided by the state. The rest comes from research grants, fees, auxiliary funds, tuition, and private gifts.

improvements were completed or started. The work added or renovated more than 5.3 million square feet of space, and subsequent development added another million square feet. The growth occurred in all parts of campus, but is most noticeable in three areas: East Campus, with construction of the $39 million School of Art, a $20 million addition to the Georgia Museum of Art, a $17 million expansion of the Student Health Center, and development of East Campus Village; South Campus, with the addition of the $30 million Coliseum Training Facility, the $40 million Paul Coverdell Center for Biomedical and Health Sciences, and the $44 million Pharmacy South building; and Central Campus, with construction of the $44 million Zell Miller Student Learning Center and the $58 million addition to the William Tate Student Center. Other major construction projects of the Adams era include the $46 million Richard Russell Building Special Collections Libraries on the western edge of campus and the $41 million Complex Carbohydrate Research Center in the Riverbend Research Site.

Much campus development has been guided by a master plan implemented in 1999; it calls for a greener, more connected, and more pedestrian-friendly campus than before, one that reflects the historic character of North Campus. Under the plan, Herty Field was converted from a parking lot into inviting green space; three parking decks were erected on the campus perimeter, and a fourth was enlarged, to divert vehicles from the interior of campus; and a street that had bisected South Campus for decades was replaced by a tree-lined mall. Seventeen rain gardens were installed to control storm runoff, and new buildings were constructed with state-of-the-art environmental and energy-saving features. In 2000, the entire 759-acre campus was designated an arboretum in order to foster management and enjoyment of the nine thousand or so trees that grace the landscape. With the creation of the Office of Sustainability and the implementation of aggressive water and energy conservation measures, the university received high marks on "green report cards" issued by national sustainability watchdog organizations.

Adams's decision in 2012 to retire as president the next year launched a national search for his successor. The search ended with the selection of Jere W. Morehead, who had been the university's senior vice president for academic affairs and provost for three years. On July 1, 2013, Morehead, a Florida native who earned a law degree from UGA in 1980 and joined the Terry College of Business in 1986 to teach legal studies, became the university's twenty-second president. He is the first alumnus and first former faculty member to hold the post since Fred Davison was appointed in 1967. Before becoming provost, Morehead held several other administrative positions including vice president for instruction, vice provost for academic affairs and director of the Honors Program. He also served as vice chair of the UGA Research Foundation, vice chair of the Georgia Athletic Association, and trustee of the UGA Foundation and the UGA Real Estate Foundation.

In 2010, UGA celebrated its 225th anniversary by looking back at its past and ahead to its future. The past is a proud story of service, contributions, and leadership. As the oldest, largest, and most comprehensive educational institution in the state, UGA sets the standard for educational excellence in Georgia. The university has played a towering role in Georgia's growth through research programs that span virtually every field of human endeavor and contribute billions of dollars to the state's economy through scientific and technological innovation and expertise. UGA enrolls many of the state's brightest young people, and its alumni are leaders in government, business, science, education, the arts, and social services. A wide-ranging public service and outreach program helps enhance the quality of life for all Georgians. Firmly established as one of the best public universities in the United States, UGA has a growing international presence that greatly benefits Georgia in today's global economy.

The university's future is envisioned in a ten-year strategic plan adopted in 2010 as part of the 225th anniversary. The plan sets an ambitious agenda: the university will build on excellence in undergraduate education and graduate and professional programs; invest in emerging areas of research; strengthen service to the state and beyond; improve campus facilities and infrastructure; and advance stewardship of natural resources and campus sustainability. But though the plan was new, its underlying principles and values were not. Those were formed by young Abraham Baldwin, who proposed that the purpose of a university is to educate citizens for their own prosperity and the betterment of society. Baldwin's vision has guided the University of Georgia for more than two and a quarter centuries and will be its beacon for advancing into the exciting frontiers of the future.

CHAPTER 2

North Campus

THE TRADITIONAL BOUNDARIES of North Campus are Broad Street on the north, Jackson Street on the east, Baldwin Street on the south, and Lumpkin Street on the west.

Of the 633 acres that John Milledge bought from Daniel Easley as the site of the university, only 37 were set aside for the campus. The rest was to be rented or sold to provide income for the fledgling school. Those 37 acres contain most of North Campus, which is listed on the National Register of Historic Places as one of the most historically significant spots in Georgia.

North Campus is where the University of Georgia came to life in the summer of 1801 when Josiah Meigs, the university's second president, oversaw construction of a log structure twenty feet square and one and a half stories high. The building stood in a clearing in a dense forest, probably near where Phi Kappa Hall stands today, and was a classroom for young men recruited from private academies in the state. Three years later, the first commencement was held in an arbor near the classroom building.

For the next hundred years, the university consisted primarily of the quadrangle between the Arch and Old College. Opened in 1806, Old College was the first permanent building, and for fifteen years served as the classroom, dining hall, and dormitory for the entire student body. Only eight other permanent buildings were constructed in North Campus before the twentieth century. The exteriors of these carefully preserved buildings reflect two of the era's common architectural styles—the dull but dignified Federal design and the stately Greek Revival style.

The famed Arch, the traditional entrance to the university, and its adjoining ornamental cast-iron fence were installed around 1858. The university paid for the iron structures with $1,000 earned from the sale of a botanical garden that was established in 1833 on university land just west of campus and south of Broad Street. Covering several acres, the garden had a greenhouse, a small lake, and more than two thousand plants, shrubs, and trees, including unusual specimens such as a cutting from a weeping willow growing at Napoleon's grave. The garden, which became Athens's first park, was a popular place for picnicking and courting, but the university had to sell it when upkeep became too costly.

The use of fireplaces and wood stoves for cooking and heating, and of candles and lanterns for light, made fire an ever-present danger during the early years of the university. Three North Campus buildings were lost to flames that could not be doused for lack of water. A wooden chapel built in 1807 burned in 1830 and was replaced two years later by the current chapel. New College, originally built in 1822, was also destroyed in 1830 and also rebuilt in 1832. A building named Science Hall, which was erected in 1897 and burned in 1903, was replaced by Terrell Hall.

The university's organized athletic program started on North Campus in the late 1800s when a baseball team, and later a football team, played on a weedy field behind Moore College. It was on this site, now known as Herty Field, that in 1892 the first intercollegiate football game in Georgia was played, with UGA beating Mercer 50-0.

Campus view, ca. 1900

Improved financial fortunes and energetic new leadership sparked a wave of campus expansion in the early twentieth century. New buildings were added to the original North Campus quad, and a second quadrangle began to develop south of Old College, eventually becoming the site of the School of Law and the Ilah Dunlap Little Library. More buildings appeared in the area west of the two quads, along with a charming ornamental garden created to commemorate the first garden club in the United States. Depression-era federal grants in the late 1930s helped fund three new buildings on the periphery of North Campus.

Only five major buildings were erected in the North Campus sector between 1950 and 2000. The last was Sanford Hall, squeezed into a spot beside Brooks Hall in 1997. With little developable space left, North Campus is likely to remain much as it is today—a scenic, gracious, and historically unique gem for the citizens of Georgia.

BROAD STREET

The Arch

THOMAS STREET

Holmes/Hunter
Academic Building
0120

Phi Kappa Hall
0020

Tanner
Building
0123

Demosthenian Hall
0021

Bernard
Ramsey
Sculpture

Terrell Hall
0023

Meigs Hall
0024

The
Chapel
Bell

The Chapel
0022

Toombs
Oak
Sundial

JACKSON STREET

Moore College
0025

Administration
Building
0631

Bishop
House
0032

Candler
Hall
0031

New College
0030

Abraham
Baldwin
Statue

Hubert B. Owens
Fountain

EAST CAMPUS ROAD

Herty
Field

Old College
0130

Lustrat
House
0632

Gilbert
Hall
0640

Presidents Club
Garden

Waddel
Hall
0041

Jackson
Street
Building
0040

Hirsch Hall
0043

Caldwell
Hall
0046

Peabody
Hall
0042

Old Athens Cemetery

Denmark
Hall
0044

Brooks
Hall
0055

Dean
Rusk
Hall
0045

orris Hall
2204

Founders
Memorial
Garden

Ilah Dunlap Little
Memorial Library
0054

Baldwin Hall
0050

Sanford
Hall
0058

LeConte
Hall
0053

Joe
Brown
Hall
0250

Park Hall
0056

Latin American
Ethnobotanical
Garden

LUMPKIN STREET

BALDWIN STREET

Walking under the Arch

A long-standing tradition forbade freshmen to walk under the Arch. According to an oft-told story, when Daniel Redfern arrived as a freshman in the early 1900s, he vowed he would not walk under the Arch until he graduated. A professor who learned of the promise spread the word among students, and the tradition was born. The prohibition came about when the student body was small enough that freshmen were easily identified and subjected to hazing rituals, including being forced to wear "rat" caps. Upperclassmen took the Arch ban seriously, posting signs and even guards at the Arch to ward off freshmen who tried to break the rule. The prohibition even gave rise to a warning that a freshman who walked under the Arch would never graduate. As enrollments grew in the late twentieth century, the tradition faded, but in recent years students have revived it by refusing to walk under the Arch until they are seniors or until they graduate.

The Arch

INSTALLED: around 1858 | LOCATION: northern rim of North Campus bordering Broad Street

The University Arch is UGA's most venerated icon and the traditional entrance to campus. Cast at the Athens Foundry from three lampposts and decorative house brackets, the Arch is patterned after the Great Seal of Georgia, with three columns representing Wisdom, Justice and Moderation—the state's motto. Originally the Arch was at sidewalk level and had wooden gates that were closed at night, but they disappeared in 1885, probably the result of a student prank. The steps leading up to the Arch were installed around 1900, and globes containing electric lights were added to the Arch in the 1940s. In 1946, the structure was moved five feet back from Broad Street in order to improve pedestrian movement. The Arch has long been a favored site for students and Athens citizens to stage demonstrations, rallies, protests, and other gatherings. In September 2001, the Arch became a spontaneous community memorial to victims of the World Trade Center attacks, bedecked with candles, flowers, and written tributes. The Arch even has its own benefactor: a university alumnus, Daniel Redfern, left a $1,000 bequest in his will with instructions that interest from the money be used to paint the Arch and keep it in good repair.

The iron fence separating the campus from Broad Street was cast at the Athens Foundry and installed about the same time as the Arch. The fence replaced a wooden fence built in 1833 to keep out animals that roamed the town's dirt streets—and to deter students from venturing into town. A fence on the western edge of North Campus along Lumpkin Street is identical in appearance to the Broad Street section, but was not installed until 1947. Damaged and weathered parts of the Broad Street fence have been replaced over the years, but the entire fence had never been taken down until the summer of 2012, when workers dismantled it for a thorough cleaning and repainting. The work included sandblasting each piece, replacing damaged parts, painting with a primer that withstands high temperatures and humidity, and anchoring the reinstalled fence in 250-pound granite footers.

Holmes/Hunter Academic Building

BUILT: 1905 | NAMED FOR: Hamilton Holmes and Charlayne Hunter-Gault, the first African Americans to enroll at UGA | CURRENT USE: Office of the Registrar, Office of Student Financial Aid, Equal Opportunity Office, Office of Institutional Diversity, Center for International Trade and Security | BUILDING 0120

This building was created by a clever architectural scheme that joined two of the university's oldest structures. The Ivy Building (so named because it was almost covered by ivy) was built on the site in 1831 to house the university's small library. In 1862, a larger building for the library, called Old Library, was

The First Library Building

The Ivy Building

completed (at a cost of $14,600) adjacent to the Ivy Building. One floor was for the library, and the building included a mineralogical museum and a lecture hall that could seat more than three hundred. The university's first female staff member, Sarah Frierson, was hired in 1888 to work here as assistant librarian. Students working in these buildings published the first edition of the *Red and Black*, the student newspaper, in November 1893. In 1905, Charles Strahan, an engineering professor and architect, devised a plan to link the buildings with a central portico and staircase. He added tall metal Corinthian columns to the front and a balustrade to the roof, creating a single structure in the then-popular Beaux-Arts architectural style. Just as the new facility, named the Academic Building, opened in 1905, the library moved to new quarters, leaving the Academic Building for classrooms, laboratories, and academic departments. It has housed the president's office and other administrative offices, including the Registrar's Office, where, in January 1961, Hamilton Holmes and Charlayne Hunter registered as UGA's first African American students. Their names were added to the building in a 2001 ceremony marking the fortieth anniversary of integration at UGA.

Demosthenian Hall

BUILT: 1824 | NAMED FOR: Demosthenian Literary Society | CURRENT USE: Demosthenian Literary Society | BUILDING 0021

Debating was a popular extracurricular activity for the university's first students, and the Demosthenian Literary Society, named for the Greek orator Demosthenes and founded in 1803, was the university's first student organization. Society members raised $4,000 to construct Demosthenian Hall, the third-oldest building on campus. The building's two-foot-thick brick walls are encased in cement. An elliptical fanlight over the doorway, topped by a Palladian window, is the only ornamentation on the austere exterior of this Federal-style building. The lower floor, now a book-lined lounge and office area, has served as a library, bookstore, and music room. Society members meet and debate in the large upper room, which has intricately carved fireplace mantels and window moldings and a ceiling with elaborate decorative plasterwork of a rare style known as "Adam medallion." The speaker's desk, dating to the 1820s, overlooks a section cut from the trunk of the historic Toombs Oak. In 1997, the building received a $200,000 renovation—financed mainly through alumni donations—which restored the top floor to its original layout and color scheme. The society, which did not admit women until the 1970s, claims among its members many notable Georgians, including governors, senators, military generals, jurists, and business tycoons.

Phi Kappa Hall

BUILT: 1836 | NAMED FOR: Phi Kappa Literary Society | CURRENT USE: Phi Kappa Literary Society and Georgia Debate Union | BUILDING 0020

The Athens lawyer Joseph Henry Lumpkin (who later became chief justice of the Georgia Supreme Court and helped start the UGA School of Law) organized the Phi Kappa Literary Society in 1820 as a rival to the Demosthenian Literary Society. The group met in various campus buildings until Lumpkin and Alexander Stephens (a UGA graduate who was later vice president of the Confederate States of America) began a fund-raising drive in 1831 that brought in enough money from members and alumni to cover the $3,500 cost of Phi Kappa Hall, the fifth-oldest building on campus. The temple-form Greek Revival structure, with four Doric columns supporting a brick-paved portico, was intentionally sited on an axis opposite to Demosthenian Hall. Originally, the large upper floor was the debate hall, and the ground floor was partitioned into a library and social rooms. The building was a quartermaster depot for provisions for the Confederate army during the Civil War, and after the war a small contingent of Union soldiers that briefly bivouacked in Athens stabled horses in the bottom floor while turning the upper floor into a "house of revelry." The society's large library was destroyed when the building was looted following its occupation. During Reconstruction, the building was headquarters of the local Freedmen's Bureau, and it has also been used as a gymnasium, computer training center, music department offices, and university bookstore. In 2005, it was extensively renovated

and returned to its original use as home of the Phi Kappa Literary Society. Rivalry between Demosthenians and Phi Kappas was once bitter enough to spark physical as well as verbal battles, but the groups are on friendlier terms today. In addition to Lumpkin and Stephens, Phi Kappa's notable members include the southern journalist Henry W. Grady, former Georgia governor Eugene Talmadge, and former governor and U.S. senator Richard B. Russell.

The Chapel

BUILT: 1832 | CURRENT USE: Venue for lectures, meetings, and concerts | BUILDING 0022

Considered by many the most beautiful building on campus, the Chapel was erected over the ruins of a wooden chapel constructed in 1807 and destroyed by fire in 1830. Built at a cost of $15,000 and designed in the classic style of a temple, the Chapel was one of the first Greek Revival structures in Athens and is said to have been the inspiration for homes built by wealthy merchants and planters of the era. With its gleaming white exterior, near perfect proportions, and six massive Doric columns, the building quickly became a centerpiece for university and community activities, including required daily religious services for students. At the time of construction, it marked the point from which

The Chapel with its cupola

the town's boundaries were measured. Inside is a giant oil painting of the interior of St. Peter's Cathedral in Rome, created by the U.S. artist George Cooke and presented to the university in 1867 by Daniel Pratt, an Alabama industrialist. Seventeen feet high and twenty-three feet long, and weighing more than a ton, the painting is so large that the building had to be altered to accommodate it. The Chapel served as a hospital for wounded Confederate soldiers during the Civil War and briefly housed more than four hundred Union prisoners. After the war, Union soldiers encamped in Athens ravaged the Chapel, breaking windows, burning benches, and using the columns for target practice. The building and painting have twice been damaged by fire, including a blaze in 1955 that required an eighteen-month restoration of the painting. In a major $300,000 renovation carried out in the mid-1990s, a new HVAC system and bathrooms were installed, the entire floor was sloped to improve visual perspective for the audience, and seats were reconditioned.

The Chapel Bell

A bell has sounded over campus since UGA's earliest days. A bell strung between two trees awakened the first students for 6:00 a.m. prayers and later marshaled them for meals, class, study periods, and bedtime. The first wooden chapel had a cast-iron bell that was destroyed when the building burned in

1830. The current Chapel was completed in 1832 with a bell in a cupola on the roof. The decaying cupola was removed in 1913 and the bell transferred to a tower behind the Chapel, where it signaled class changes into the 1950s. During World War II, the bell briefly was Athens's air raid "siren." It has chimed for funerals, weddings, holidays, and other special events, and each spring it tolls in a somber ceremony of remembrance for students, faculty members, and staff members, who died in the previous year. The tradition of ringing the bell to celebrate football victories dates to the 1890s, when freshmen were required to ring it until midnight—unless Georgia beat Georgia Tech, in which case it could ring until morning. The current, seven-hundred-pound bronze bell was cast in Medway, Massachusetts, in 1835. When and why it got to Athens is uncertain, but it is believed to have been installed in the Chapel cupola between 1903 and 1911. It was preceded by at least two other bells, which were retired after they cracked. Over the years, Chapel bells have been vandalized by pranksters who painted them with slogans, stole the clapper, cut the bell rope, and even tried to steal the bell itself. It has fallen several times, either as a result of pranks or overly exuberant ringing. In 2007, jubilant Bulldog football fans rang it so hard following a Georgia victory over Florida that it fell out of its moorings in the tower. The accident revealed the eighty-four-year-old tower to be unsafe, and the bell was removed and the tower dismantled. Workers built the current forty-foot tower, almost identical to the original, in time for the bell to ring after the first game of the 2008 football season. In 2011, the Chapel bell became the centerpiece of a UGA public service announcement shown during televised football games. The spot, created by four alumni, features the bell loudly tolling behind the R.E.M. song "Oh My Heart."

Toombs Oak Sundial

The ornate sundial in front of the Chapel marks the spot where a tree known as the Toombs Oak once grew and spawned one of the university's most enduring legends.

Robert Toombs served as a U.S. congressman and senator from Georgia before the Civil War and as secretary of state of the Confederacy and brigadier general during the war; he helped write a new state constitution after the war. But none of his future success could have been foretold when Toombs arrived at UGA in 1824 as a rowdy fourteen-year-old freshman. The university's strict

Campus Trees

Perhaps fittingly for a campus hewn from a forest, trees have always been a prominent feature of UGA's landscape. The iconic grace and beauty of North Campus is defined by majestic oaks, elms, and poplars that hark back to the university's beginning, when Josiah Meigs taught the first classes in a clearing beneath giant trees while workers finished a classroom built with logs cut from the dense forest. Early North Campus buildings probably were limited to two or three stories in order to take advantage of the forest's cooling shade.

As trees were cut for construction and fuel, replacement saplings were planted. A border of trees was planted in 1824 to separate North Campus from Broad Street, and in 1830 a number of trees were set out in the North Campus quad, including chinaberries, black locusts, and a tree called ailanthus, imported from the Moluccas in the East Indies. Students in later years reviled the trees, describing the chinaberry as "having no virtue at all except to furnish berries to the robins," and derisively calling the ailanthuses "trees of heaven" for their "sickening odor." Most of the objectionable trees were removed in a major landscaping in 1881 that added some four hundred new trees to North Campus.

Students in the early days expressed dislike for faculty members and politicians by hanging them in effigy from North Campus trees. Graduating classes in the 1870s planted a tree as part of their commencement ceremony, in which the male students held hands while walking around a sapling, singing songs, and puffing a peace pipe.

Also in the 1870s, an Athens businessman named Young L. G. Harris set out five oak trees along the iron fence at the edge of North Campus, and later he planted willow oaks in a grove at the northwest corner of North Campus where Broad and Lumpkin Streets intersect. These may be some of the oldest existing trees on campus, though no one knows for certain, since disease, wind, and ice regularly take their toll on some of the largest and oldest trees. In 2009, an Oconee County nursery, Select Trees, announced a donation of more than one thousand trees, worth more than $1 million, to UGA in honor of internationally known university horticulturist Michael Dirr and his wife, Bonnie.

Today, an estimated nine thousand trees dot the main campus, many thriving in green spaces such as Founders Memorial Garden and Old Athens Cemetery on North Campus, and small forested areas behind Clarke Howell Hall and the Driftmier Engineering Center on South Campus. In 2000, the entire campus was designated an arboretum in order to promote the maintenance, enjoyment and study of trees. The arboretum's walking tour of trees lists 154 labeled species, including common native trees such as magnolias, red oaks, white oaks, and beeches, along with such exotic varieties as the blue Atlas cedar, native to the Atlas Mountains of North Africa; the Chinese parasol tree and royal paulownia, originally from China; and the Japanese zelkova and Japanese black pine. The Arbor Day Foundation has designated UGA a Tree Campus USA in recognition of its sustained commitment to the care, health, and educational use of trees.

rules required students to be studious, decorous, and pious. Toombs had none of the desired qualities. He chewed tobacco, drank liquor, cursed, gambled, and skipped mandatory vespers. After a brawl in which he tried, over the course of two days, to attack a pair of brothers with a bowl, a knife, a hatchet, a pistol, a club, and his fists, he was expelled. After being readmitted through a petition to the faculty, he resumed his troublesome ways, and by January 1828, in his senior year, his excesses had become so intolerable that the faculty permanently dismissed him. According to the legend, on the day he would have graduated he stood under a large oak tree in front of the Chapel, where commencement was held, and delivered his own graduation speech with such eloquence that the audience left the Chapel and gathered outside to listen to him.

The tree, which became known as the Toombs Oak, was supposedly struck by lightning and killed just moments before Toombs himself died in 1885.

Like many legends, this one combines fact with fiction. Toombs was expelled, and there was a large oak in front of the Chapel. But he never gave his own graduation speech beneath it. The story may have been concocted by the journalist Henry W. Grady, a friend of Toombs, for one of Grady's famous speeches. And lightning did knock out the tree's top—but in 1884, more than a year before Toombs's death. Toombs eventually graduated from Union College, studied law in Virginia, and returned to Georgia, where he was admitted to the bar and embarked on his political career. Though years later he reportedly refused to accept a degree from UGA, he became a staunch supporter of the school, serving on the board of trustees from 1859 until he died.

When the tree trunk finally collapsed from decay in 1908, students placed a sundial where it had stood, to commemorate Toombs and the oak. In 1971, the sundial face disappeared ("missing, possibly stolen," according to police records), but the pedestal remained. In 2008, a century after the first sundial was placed, a new face, similar in size and appearance to the original, was installed on the pedestal. The new face was commissioned by descendants of J. Howard Neisler, president of the Class of 1908.

Terrell Hall

BUILT: 1904 | NAMED FOR: William Terrell, an early supporter of agricultural research at UGA | CURRENT USE: Office of Undergraduate Admissions | BUILDING 0023

Terrell Hall was built atop the preserved basement walls of a building named Science Hall, which was erected in 1897 and gutted by fire on November 19, 1903 (Science Hall's cornerstone is visible at Terrell's northwest corner).

Science Hall housed the Chemistry, Biology, and Pharmacy Departments
and the office of Chancellor Walter Hill. A $20,000 appropriation from
the Georgia General Assembly, along with fire insurance proceeds, enabled
the university to quickly erect Terrell Hall, which was designed by Charles
Strahan, a professor of civil engineering and mathematics who also designed
the Holmes/Hunter Academic Building. Constructed nearly a century after
the first permanent building opened, Terrell deviated from the traditional
architecture of North Campus: its Romanesque design reflected architectural
trends of the time such as the arched entrance and window openings, a low-
pitched roof, and a prominent cornice. Terrell Hall housed the Chemistry
Department and Pharmacy School for many years as well as air force ROTC.
Before an extensive renovation in the early 1990s, Terrell was home to the
University of Georgia Press, the Office of Public Information, and the Carl
Vinson Institute of Government.

William Terrell was a wealthy antebellum planter and surgeon who served in
the Georgia legislature and represented the state in Congress from 1817 to 1821.
Keenly interested in scientific research and agriculture, he gave UGA $20,000
in state bonds in 1854 to endow a professorial chair in agricultural chemistry.
The gift—the university's first endowed faculty position and one of the first
endowed chairs of agriculture in the country—planted the seed for the expansive agricultural program that emerged at UGA in the next century.

I spent four wonderful years at the University of Georgia. The football games were phenomenal; we went 43–4–1 during my years at the university, winning three SEC titles and a national championship, and played in four New Year's Day bowl games. I got to see the greatest football play in Georgia history ("Lindsay Scott! Lindsay Scott! Lindsay Scott!") and the greatest player in NCAA history, Herschel Walker. Even basketball was amazing, as the Dawgs went to their only Final Four ever. I voted in my first election, drank my first beer, and met some lifelong friends in Athens. But my best memory is of a single quiet evening walking a dog on North Campus.

My senior year at Georgia, my mother's Yorkie, a rambunctious little thing named Whistle, was at the UGA vet school for some tests. My girlfriend, Daphne, and I took her out of the vet school for a walk one night on North Campus, near the Arch. As we sat on the wrought-iron bench there, the dog twisting anxiously on the leash, I dropped to one knee and asked Daphne to marry me. I knew that bench would be there long after I was gone, and I wanted to be able to take our children by that spot years later and say to them, "See that bench? That's where I asked your mother to marry me."

Daphne accepted, of course—this wouldn't be a good memory if she hadn't. Since then, Daphne's had cancer twice, but she survived despite all odds, and we've raised two sons together. Josh and Chris grew up coming to Athens on fall Saturdays. They've seen the famous North Campus bench many times. They've heard this story over and over. And, at least for me, it never gets old, because that single moment changed my entire life forever.

Marrying Daphne is still the best thing I ever did. And it all started with that one night on North Campus.

Mark E. Murphy, Class of 1984

New College

BUILT: 1832 | CURRENT USE: Office of the Vice President for Instruction, Office of Academic Fiscal Affairs, Office of Faculty Affairs, Office of Academic Planning | BUILDING 0030

This building stands on the ruins of the original New College, the university's third building, constructed in 1822 as a residence hall. The four-story structure burned to the ground on a cold December night in 1830. Students escaped unharmed, though the following spring a boy was killed when bricks from a ruined wall fell on him. The building was quickly rebuilt—minus the fourth floor—and reopened in 1832. Designed in the New England Colonial architecture style, it was one of the first structures in Athens to have steel reinforcements, known as hurricane bars, between the floors as protection against natural disasters. In 2009, workers carrying out a major restoration unearthed numerous artifacts believed to be from the original building, including wrought-iron nails, blown-glass bottles, glazed cookware, and a pottery bowl that may date to the late prehistoric Lamar period (AD 1350–1600), when Native Americans lived in the area. They also found remnants of a mysterious brick structure below the level of the original building. Though the building's exterior appears to be stone, it is actually stucco scored to resemble stone blocks. In addition to serving as a dorm and classrooms, New College has been used as a library, post office, and bookstore. From 1930 until the 1950s, it housed a popular snack bar called the Co-op. It has also housed a number of administrative and academic units, including the colleges of pharmacy, education, and arts and sciences.

Administration Building

BUILT: 1905 | CURRENT USE: Offices of the university president and other senior administrators | BUILDING 0631

Financed by a $50,000 gift from the philanthropist George Foster Peabody, the building opened in 1905 as UGA's new library. Constructed just two years after the Science Hall fire, it was the first university building designed to be fireproof. Its unique features include the names of classic literary figures engraved on the exterior copper frieze. Originally housing sixty thousand volumes, the building was expanded in 1937 to hold a growing book collection that eventually totaled more than two hundred thousand volumes. The Georgia Museum of Art occupied the library basement from 1945, when the museum was started, until 1952, when the library moved to new quarters. The museum then expanded into the entire building and remained there until moving in 1996 to its new facility on East Campus. The building then underwent an extensive renovation designed to recapture its historical ambiance and highlight its original architectural features. The restored building, opened in 2000, features rich colors and traditional woodwork and includes an original skylight and replicas of original staircases in the main lobby. Other features include decorative scrolled-plaster cornice work, period furnishings, and a collection of portraits of university presidents.

George Foster Peabody didn't set foot on the UGA campus until he was forty-eight years old, but became the university's greatest benefactor in the early twentieth century. Born in Columbus, Georgia, in 1852, Peabody moved with his parents to Brooklyn, New York, in 1865 and went on to make a fortune as an investment banker by financing railroad construction and developing the company that became General Electric. Peabody first visited UGA in 1901, when his friend Oscar Straus, a Georgian who cofounded Macy's department store, was invited by UGA chancellor Walter Hill to speak at the university's centennial celebration. Peabody came along and struck up an instant friendship with Hill. Soon Peabody—who was deeply committed to education and was already donating to other schools—began giving money to UGA. In 1902, he donated $50,000 (and a large number of books) for the library building that is now the Administration Building. Two years later, he underwrote most of the expenses for Hill and a group of state leaders to travel to the University of Wisconsin and Cornell University to learn about agricultural education programs at those schools. Over subsequent years, he made additional gifts to UGA that eventually totaled some $250,000, far surpassing any individual private support the university had ever received. Along

UGA *Memory*

It was 2001, I had just been accepted to UGA, and it was a week before classes started. I decided to go jogging through North Campus. The weather was really cool that morning, and the sky was clear. I remember looking between two buildings on North Campus as I was jogging. The sun was coming up, and this overwhelming feeling came over me. It felt really good. It was like the sun telling me, "Here is your new beginning at this wonderful school. Enjoy it and do your best." I love you UGA.

Douglas Kaliher, Class of 2005

with his donations, Peabody advised both Hill and his successor, Chancellor David Barrow, on many initiatives to improve the university. He was made a life trustee of the university by a special legislative act, and he received honorary degrees from UGA, Harvard, and Washington and Lee University. In 1938, the year he died, the Henry Grady School of Journalism created an award to recognize outstanding radio broadcasting and named the prize for Peabody in appreciation of his support for the university.

Abraham Baldwin Statue

This statue, erected in 2011, honors the man who wrote the charter that created the University of Georgia and who served as the university's first president. The sculptors Teena Stern and Don Haugen of Marietta created the statue after studying historic paintings, including a famous painting of the signers of the U.S. Constitution. The bronze statue—seven feet six inches high and weighing four hundred pounds—was financed largely by the UGA Alumni Association, with a lead gift from Ted Mullins.

Born in Guilford, Connecticut, Abraham Baldwin arrived in Georgia around 1783 after having studied theology and taught at Yale College, served as a chaplain in the Revolutionary War, and earned a license to practice law. Strongly interested in education, he may have been drawn to Georgia by the educational opportunities that could be developed in a state with only a few small private academies. In addition to playing a key role in creating UGA and signing the U.S Constitution, he served in the U.S. House of Representatives for ten years and—after helping find a site for UGA in 1801 and resigning as president—he served in the U.S. Senate until he died in 1807 at the age of fifty-three. He is buried near Washington, D.C. It is not known whether he ever returned to Athens to see the university he created. In 1985, as part of the university's bicentennial celebration, the U.S. Postal Service issued an Abraham Baldwin stamp. Baldwin Hall and Baldwin Street on campus are named for him, as is the Abraham Baldwin Agricultural College in Tifton and Baldwin County in Georgia.

Old College

BUILT: 1806 | CURRENT USE: Franklin College of Arts and Sciences | BUILDING 0130

Old College is the university's first permanent building, the oldest building in Athens, and one of the oldest in Northeast Georgia. The committee appointed in 1801 to find a location for the university was instructed to contract for a building that would house one hundred students. But it was not until 1803 that university trustees sold enough land to raise the $1,200 needed to pay Captain Jett Thomas to construct the building. Josiah Meigs, the university's second president, brought the blueprints of a building at Yale named Connecticut Hall when he came to Georgia, and UGA's sturdy, no-frills structure closely resembles that building. Officials had to negotiate a

The Immortal
Summey Hall Biscuits

Stories abound about the escapades of rambunctious young residents of Old College
when it was a dormitory. One tale recounted
by the longtime university registrar Thomas
Reed in his history of the university concerns
biscuits baked by "Aunt Jane" Summey. Mrs.
Summey and her husband, Peter, served as
house parents in the 1880s, temporarily giving
Old College the nickname Summey Hall. The
biscuits, according to Reed, were so thin, dry,
and hard that the boys wouldn't eat them.
Instead, they secretly took them to a room,
where they strung them on pieces of wire or
cord, eventually stockpiling more than two
thousand biscuits. Deciding that the campus
needed decorating for an upcoming commencement, some boys set to work in the dark
of night. The next morning, ropes of hard,
stale biscuits wreathed the Arch, hung from
trees, and entwined the Chapel's columns.
Reed says he preserved two biscuits in brown
wrapping paper and kept them in a trunk for
twenty-three years. When he finally threw
them out into his garden, they were harder
than wood but showed no sign of decay, leading him to term them "immortal." He specu-
lated that an archaeologist would one day
find them "and write some learned treatise
on the peculiar coins used by Americans in
those days."

treaty with the Cherokee in order to haul in construction materials, including lime from Tennessee, nails from Augusta, and bricks from a factory several miles away. Because they didn't know in which direction the campus
would grow, designers made the back and front of the building identical. As
originally constructed, Old College had twenty-four rooms spread over three
floors, with four tall chimneys serving fireplaces in each room. Ninety-six windows provided good ventilation but little protection from cold Georgia win-
ters. Here the university's entire early student body—a small group of young
men—lived, ate meals, and studied Latin, Greek, science, and mathematics.
Originally called Franklin College (in honor of Benjamin Franklin), the building took on the name Old College as more buildings were constructed and
it became strictly a dormitory. Among Old College residents were Alexander
Stephens and his roommate Crawford Long, who pioneered the use of ether as
anesthesia.

   During the Civil War, the building served as a Confederate hospital and
housed refugees from Charleston, Savannah, and New Orleans. Wear and tear
by rowdy male residents, and damage inflicted by Union soldiers after the Civil
War, so deteriorated the building that by 1908 mortar holding the original
brick walls together was crumbling, and the structure was on the verge of

collapse. It was saved from demolition by a special $10,000 appropriation from the General Assembly to replace the original walls and reinforce the roof. During World War II, the U.S. Navy took over the building for a preflight training school, named it Ranger Hall, and extensively reconfigured the interior to serve as cadet barracks. After the war, the building was renovated to house administrative offices, including the president's office. In 2005, work began on a major rehabilitation that included installing central heat and air, adding an elevator and a ramp, raising ceilings to their original height, and creating a high-tech classroom. The work ended with a ceremony in 2006 marking the building's bicentennial and returning it to its original purpose—housing the Franklin College of Arts and Sciences. A marble plaque on the north wall that commemorates the siting of the building on July 7, 1801, may have been installed when the building was originally completed.

Hubert B. Owens Fountain

BUILT: 1989 | NAMED FOR: Hubert B. Owens, professor and dean of environmental design

During forty-five years on the UGA faculty, Hubert Owens pioneered landscape architecture education in Georgia and became a leading figure in the field of environmental design. Born in 1905 in Canon, Georgia, Owens earned bachelor's and master's degrees at UGA and did graduate work at Columbia, Cornell, and Harvard. Starting from a single landscape architecture course in 1928, he built a full program of study that in 1969 became the School of Environmental Design (now the College of Environment and Design), for which he served as founding dean. The first landscape architect for the Georgia Highway Department, he was instrumental in creating and developing the Founders Memorial Garden on campus and was the primary landscape designer for UGA's North Campus. In the 1940s, Owens proposed a garden on the east side of Old College with a water feature. But there was only enough money to build a small plaza. When the deteriorating plaza was rebuilt in 1989, the university's physical plant revived Owens's idea and installed the first fountain on campus in his honor.

Lustrat House

BUILT: 1847 | NAMED FOR: Joseph Lustrat, head of the department of Romance languages | CURRENT USE: Office of Legal Affairs | BUILDING 0632

In its early years, the university built several faculty residences on campus so that professors could supervise student behavior—a common requirement for faculty members at the time. Lustrat House, the seventh-oldest building on campus, is the only remaining faculty house on the North Campus quad. Built originally on a spot north of its present location, it was moved in 1905 to make way for the new library (now the Administration Building).

The first resident was John LeConte, a professor of natural history. Charles Morris, an English professor and a former major in the Confederate army, and his family lived here in the early 1880s. The last occupant was Joseph Lustrat, who lived in the house from 1897 until he died in 1927. A native of France, Lustrat came to UGA with a law degree from the Sorbonne but spent thirty years teaching languages. The building served for a time as a house museum for paintings and furnishings owned by Ilah Dunlap Little, benefactor of UGA's main library, and for several years it was the office of the university president.

Waddel Hall

BUILT: 1821 | NAMED FOR: Moses Waddel, UGA president, 1819–29 | CURRENT USE: Office of Special Events | BUILDING 0041

The second-oldest building on campus and one of the smallest, Waddel Hall is named for the university's fifth president, the first southerner to hold the office. When Waddel, a North Carolina native and graduate of Hampden-Sydney College in Virginia, arrived, UGA was nearly defunct, with only seven students and three professors. An energetic leader and inspiring teacher, but a strict authoritarian, he reinvigorated the school by increasing enrollment, improving finances, and imposing a stringent student disciplinary code. This plain Federal-style structure, the first of three buildings erected during Waddel's presidency, originally had a chapel on the ground floor and was called Philosophical Hall because the second floor contained books, a laboratory, and equipment for the sciences, or "natural philosophy." In the 1870s, it was the headquarters of the State College of Agriculture and Mechanic Arts and was called Agricultural Hall. It has been reconfigured for many uses, including classrooms, a gymnasium, a boardinghouse, and offices of the university press.

For much of the early part of the twentieth century, it was the home of Thomas Reed, the university's longtime registrar. Named for Waddel in the 1950s, it served from 1977 until 1996 as the office of law professor and former U.S. secretary of state Dean Rusk and as headquarters of the Rusk Center for International and Comparative Law. Rusk hosted many notable visitors at the building, including Lady Bird Johnson, the widow of former President Lyndon Johnson; former secretary of state Henry Kissinger; and former president Jimmy Carter.

Early on the morning of January 30, 1918, when Waddel Hall was a private boardinghouse, a twenty-year-old man shot and killed a seventeen-year-old woman and then killed himself in a room in the building. The man and woman were from Jefferson, and neither was a UGA student. The man left a suicide note indicating he was depressed and unhappy, but gave no reason or motive for the incident, which is believed to be the first homicide on campus.

Presidents Club Garden

BUILT: 1973 | NAMED FOR: presidents of UGA | CURRENT USE: scenic spot for relaxation

Though gifts from private donors are today an essential source of funding, the university was a latecomer to organized fund-raising. While many other large institutions had staffs of professional fund-raisers, the solicitation of private gifts at UGA was carried out mainly by the Alumni Society or informally by the president, deans, and other officials. In 1973 an office of Development and University Relations was established to manage fund-raising, along with alumni, public relations, and special events programs. One of the early fund-raising initiatives was the Presidents Club, which recognized donors who made or pledged a lifetime gift of $10,000—at the time the highest giving level. Named to honor all the presidents of the university, the club gave members special privileges, such as invitations to exclusive social events and preferential treatment for academic and athletic activities. Elmer Schacht, an Athens businessman and member of the club, funded this scenic garden to publicly recognize those generous benefactors. Plaques representing more than two thousand households were installed on the brick wall between 1973 and 1994, when the club's name became Annual Presidents Club, since the criteria for membership were changed to require an annual donation of at least $1,000. The garden, which is inviting year-round with greenery and seasonal flowers, is a popular spot for studying, socializing, and relaxing.

UGA *Memory*

When I met my future husband, Wayne, on campus in 1975, there was a large gnarled tree where the Presidents Club Garden is now located, behind Old College. Whenever we arranged to meet between classes, it was always at that tree. I would sit on a low-growing branch that had a metal stake under it for support (leading me to believe I wasn't the only person who sat there!). After our wedding in 1976, Wayne's parents prepared a romantic post-wedding dinner for the newlyweds, setting a table for two with our china and crystal at our favorite place on campus, under this wonderful tree. When I learned years later that the tree had been cut down because of disease, I told my mother about my sadness at losing a part of campus so sentimental to me. She replied that she had recently seen a photo of the tree, taken by a student who thought it was strikingly unusual. Two weeks later, she presented me with an eight-by-ten photo of "our" tree, photographed before it was cut down! That photo, symbolizing our courtship, now hangs on the wall between our UGA diplomas.

Carol Stansell Nobles, Class of 1977; MEd, 1979
Ronald Wayne Nobles, Class of 1976

Displayed throughout the law school are
portraits of former deans and faculty, noted
alumni, and other famous Georgians. Among
the portraits are those of four Georgians who
served on the U.S. Supreme Court, including John A. Campbell, the only UGA graduate
to serve on the Court. Campbell, born near
Washington, Georgia, received a bachelor's
degree in 1826, long before the law school was
established, and was admitted to the State Bar
of Georgia in 1829 after reading law with John
Clark, a UGA graduate and former Georgia
governor. Campbell moved to Alabama, where
he practiced law until President Franklin
Pierce, at the urging of several sitting Supreme
Court justices, appointed him to the Court
in 1853. He resigned in 1861 and was assistant
secretary of war for the Confederacy in the
Civil War. After the war, he practiced law in
New Orleans and argued a number of cases
before the Supreme Court. Another Georgian,
Joseph R. Lamar, attended UGA from 1873 to
1875, but graduated from Bethany College. He
was appointed to the Supreme Court from
Georgia in 1911, serving until 1916.

Hirsch Hall

BUILT: 1932 | NAMED FOR: Harold Hirsch, a major supporter of the School of Law |
CURRENT USE: UGA School of Law | BUILDING 0043

The university began offering instruction in law in 1843, and the School of
Law was founded in 1859 as UGA's second school, after the Franklin College
of Arts and Sciences. The school was started by the prominent Athens lawyers Thomas R. R. Cobb, Joseph Henry Lumpkin, and William Hope Hull,
who taught the first classes in their law offices, several blocks from campus.
In 1867, the school moved onto campus in the Ivy Building (later to become
the Academic Building), then in 1919 moved back off campus to a now-
demolished building that stood across Broad Street from North Campus.
An alumni fund drive raised $80,000 to build and furnish Hirsch Hall,
named for Harold Hirsch, a UGA graduate (Class of 1901) who became general counsel and vice president of the Coca-Cola Company and was a major
benefactor of the university. Designed in traditional Georgian Colonial
style, the building is topped by a cupola with the scales of justice above. The
lobby, which offers a dramatic view up through the cupola, features a spiral
marble staircase with a metal balustrade. A second-floor courtroom provides
practice space for the school's nationally respected moot court and mock
trial teams.

   Originally, the entire third floor was a law library named for Alexander
Campbell King, a former U.S. solicitor general and judge of the U.S.
Fifth Circuit Court of Appeals, whose widow contributed $20,000 for
construction of the building. In 1967, the King Library moved into a large
addition to the north side of Hirsch Hall that was made possible largely
through the efforts of Governor Carl Sanders, a 1948 law school graduate.
Sanders, who was governor from 1963 to 1967, was instrumental in providing
state funding for the expansion and later secured a $1 million state
appropriation to buy books for the library. He made a personal gift to create
a fund to support the library, to which he donated his gubernatorial papers
and memorabilia. The reading room in the library is named for Sanders.

   An annex to the library, connected by an overhead bridge, opened in 1981
and is named for J. Alton Hosch, dean of the school from 1935 to 1964. U.S.
Supreme Court justice Hugo Black spoke at the dedication of the expansion
in 1967, and Justice Harry Blackmun spoke at the dedication of the annex.
Many notable Georgia leaders have graduated from the law school including
ten governors, six U.S. senators, many congressmen, more than a dozen

Robert Benham

Robert Benham, the first African American appointed to the Georgia Supreme Court and the first to serve as chief justice of the Supreme Court, graduated from the UGA School of Law in 1970.

justices of the Georgia Supreme Court, and numerous other state government officials. Georgia Law, as the school is known, is ranked as one of the nation's top public law schools.

Peabody Hall

BUILT: 1913 | NAMED FOR: George Peabody | CURRENT USE: Departments of Religion and Philosophy, Institute of Native American Studies | BUILDING 0042

UGA has had two important benefactors named George Peabody. One was George Foster Peabody, a major university supporter in the early twentieth century. The George Peabody for whom Peabody Hall is named was a wealthy nineteenth-century New England merchant. After the Civil War, and before his death in 1869, he established a $2.25 million fund to be dispersed over time to promote public education in the South. In the early twentieth century, UGA received $40,000 from the fund, which it used to construct this building for the School of Education, formerly housed in New College.

The original building had classrooms for shop, manual arts, and rural education as well as such traditional subjects as principles of teaching and the philosophy of education. Although all education students at the time were male, planners evidently anticipated the eventual admission of women (which

occurred five years later) by including laboratory kitchens and dining rooms in the building. The basement contained an armory for the military department. The School of Education remained in Peabody until 1962, when it moved across Jackson Street to Baldwin Hall.

Ilah Dunlap Little Memorial Library

BUILT: 1952 | NAMED FOR: Ilah Dunlap Little, library benefactor | CURRENT USE: UGA's Main Library; University of Georgia Press and the *Georgia Review* | BUILDING 0054

With the university's original motto, "To teach and to inquire into the nature of things," boldly inscribed in Latin above the front entrance, this building, commonly called the Main Library, is the heart of a network of campus libraries that together contain the largest, most comprehensive collection of research materials in Georgia. Other libraries include the Law Library, adjacent to the School of Law; the Science Library on South Campus; the Richard Russell Building Special Collections Library in the northwest quadrant of campus; an electronic library in the Zell Miller Student Learning Center; and specialized collections in the School of Music and College of Education. Collectively, these facilities contain more than 4.5 million books, more than 6.5 million microforms, and thousands of serials, manuscripts, photographs, newspapers, and other documents.

The original Main Library building, four stories tall with two basement levels, replaced a library built in 1905, which was in what is now the Administration Building. Designed in the neoclassical style by Alfred Githens, a noted library architect, the new building was funded by a $400,000 bequest from Ilah Dunlap Little, the wife of John Dozier Little, a UGA graduate (Class of 1888), state legislator, and prominent Atlanta attorney. Mrs. Little, who died in 1939, made her bequest with specific stipulations: the building had to be of red brick, had to be erected on the site of the former home of the university chancellor, and had to face north toward Old College. It also had to have white columns on all sides. Mrs. Little's gift was inadequate to fully fund the facility, and it was not until the state appropriated $1.5 million in 1949 that work could begin. Even the additional state funds were insufficient to completely carry out Mrs. Little's wishes. Only the massive Doric columns on the building's front are real; those around the sides are ornamental. Githens designed the building with several architectural features that were novel at the time, including nonpermanent, flexible walls and ninety hollow steel columns that doubled as air-conditioning ducts. The building held three hundred thousand

UGA *Press and the* Georgia Review

The University of Georgia Press, founded in 1938, and the *Georgia Review*, first published in 1947, have made UGA a fountainhead of literary excellence in the South. From Pulitzer Prize–winning authors to writers published for the first time, the Press and *Review* have presented works by many of the nation's leading scholars, fiction writers, poets, essayists, and artists. The Press, Georgia's oldest and largest book publisher and the only scholarly publisher in the University System of Georgia, issues 80–85 new books annually. Its fifteen hundred titles in print cover a wide range of topics: American history, African American studies, natural history, environmental history, international affairs, southern studies, and urban studies. The Press sponsors several nationally recognized competitions and series, including the Flannery O'Connor Award for Short Fiction, the Cave Canem Poetry Prize, and the National Poetry series. A founding partner of the online *New Georgia Encyclopedia*, the Press received the Governor's Award in the Humanities in 2008, and the Press and its authors and designers have won scores of national and regional literary and design prizes.

The quarterly *Georgia Review*, with compelling fiction, incisive criticism, evocative poetry, probing essays, and stunning artwork, has built a reputation for presenting the best in contemporary thought, writing, and visual art. The *Review* publishes established writers such as Pulitzer winners Rita Dove, Stephen Dunn, Philip Schultz, and Philip Levine, and is known for introducing bright newcomers such as Mary Hood, Todd Boss, T. C. Boyle, and Lee K. Abbott. Expertly printed on fine paper, the *Review* is a showcase for visual art and photography, presenting impeccably reproduced works by well-known and emerging painters, sculptors, and photographers. Stories, essays, and other works from the *Review* are regularly reprinted in "best of" anthologies, and the journal has amassed dozens of honors, including the top prize in the National Magazine Awards for both fiction and essay. It has been a finalist for the award eighteen times in various categories, including General Excellence. The *Review* has won in every category of the GAMMA awards, which are sponsored by the Magazine Association of the Southeast, including several General Excellence prizes. The *Review* received the Governor's Award in the Humanities in 2007.

volumes when it opened, but was designed for eventual expansion. In 1974 a seven-story annex was added, making the existing 345,605-square-foot structure the third-largest building at UGA and the largest on North Campus.

The Main Library contains materials related to art, the humanities, social sciences, business, music, and government. It holds a major newspaper collection and a map collection that includes more than 611,000 maps, air photos and imagery, atlases, and digital spatial data. The media department includes educational documentaries, classic cinema, popular movies and television shows, and international titles. In addition to physical materials, the libraries subscribe to more than 48,000 electronic journals and more than 370 research databases, and users can access 400,000 full-text e-books. The UGA libraries also host the Digital Library of Georgia, an online connection to a million digitized books, manuscripts, photographs, government documents, newspapers, and other resources at sixty other institutions and one hundred government agencies throughout Georgia. Many of the online materials are accessible through the libraries' website (www.libs.uga.edu) or through GALILEO, the statewide electronic library (www.libs.uga.edu/research). The Main Library, Science Library, and Miller Learning Center Library have computing stations for use by the public (log-in credentials are available at security desks).

Dean Rusk Hall

BUILT: 1996 | NAMED FOR: Dean Rusk, U.S. secretary of state in the Kennedy and Johnson administrations and UGA law professor. | CURRENT USE: Dean Rusk Center for International and Comparative Law, Institute of Continuing Judicial Education, other School of Law programs | BUILDING 0045

Dean Rusk helped guide the U.S. through many international crises of the mid-twentieth century, including the Bay of Pigs invasion, the Cuban missile crisis, and the Vietnam War. He joined the law school faculty in 1970 and remained associated with the school until his death in 1994. His presence helped attract many eminent scholars and prominent government figures to campus. He was instrumental in developing UGA's Center for International Trade and Security, Center for Global Policy Studies, and the Dean Rusk Center for International and Comparative Law, which fosters scholarship on pressing global concerns such as disarmament, human rights, trade, and maritime law. The Louis B. Sohn International Law Library in this building contains an extensive collection of books and monographs from the personal library of Sohn, a law professor who was a leading authority on international law. The Institute of Continuing Judicial Education uses an electronic courtroom to train Georgia judges and their staffs in use of modern legal technology. The courtroom includes cameras for taping proceedings; a video visualizer to project documents and exhibits onto a screen; and graphics imaging software to reconstruct crime and accident scenes. The building's elegant boardroom is named for Governor Carl Sanders.

LeConte Hall

BUILT: 1938 | NAMED FOR: John and Joseph LeConte, noted nineteenth-century
scientists | CURRENT USE: Department of History | BUILDING 0053

This is the second UGA building to bear the LeConte name. The first was the
building now known as Meigs Hall, which was called LeConte Hall when
it opened in 1905 to house science departments. When those departments
vacated the building in 1937, it was renamed for Josiah Meigs, UGA's second
president, and the LeConte name was transferred to this building, which was
erected with PWA funds and initially housed biological sciences departments.
The History Department has been here since 1958.

John LeConte graduated from UGA in 1838, and his brother, Joseph, in 1841.
After earning medical degrees in New York City, the brothers returned to UGA
as science professors, but found themselves in conflict with the conservative
views of President Alonzo Church, who objected to their desire to conduct
research and publish scientific findings and to their refusal to monitor student behavior. Following a fractious public dispute, they left UGA in the 1850s
and, after the Civil War, moved to California. John helped start the University
of California at Berkeley and served as its first president. Joseph was an internationally known scholar in the fields of optics, geology, and evolutionary the-
ory and helped found the Sierra Club.

Latin American Ethnobotanical Garden

BUILT: 1998 | CURRENT USE: Research and teaching related to medicinal plants

This quiet, scenic garden is a living laboratory for teaching and research in the field of ethnobotany, which deals with the relationship between people and plants. It was created by Brent and Elois Ann Berlin, professors in the Anthropology Department's ethnobiology laboratories, to study plants used for medicinal purposes by people in highland Chiapas, Mexico. The garden harbors some 150 culturally important plants found throughout Latin America and the Caribbean, as well as Georgia trees and shrubs that were important to native peoples of the southeastern Piedmont region. Students and faculty from throughout the university use the garden to study such subjects as ecological anthropology, ethnomedicine, and plant classification. The Latin American and Caribbean Studies Institute, which manages the garden, encourages local schools and other organizations to use it for instruction in social and life sciences and for learning about the importance of medicinal plants. The garden is also a popular spot for meetings, small concerts, and receptions.

Meigs Hall

BUILT: 1905 | NAMED FOR: Josiah Meigs, UGA president, 1801–10 | CURRENT USE: Institute of Higher Education | BUILDING 0024

Josiah Meigs, UGA's second president, is also the second person to be the namesake of this building. Designed by Charles Strahan, the engineering professor who designed the Holmes/Hunter Academic Building and Terrell Hall, the building was partially paid for with surplus funds from the construction of Terrell Hall. When it opened as home of the Biology and Zoology Departments, it was named LeConte Hall in honor of John and Joseph LeConte, UGA graduates and teachers who left the university because of a feud with the president and became prominent scientists in the late nineteenth century. When the science departments moved to new quarters in 1937, the Psychology Department moved into the building and it was renamed for Meigs, who succeeded Abraham Baldwin as president and taught UGA's first class in 1801. From 1969 to 1999, the building was occupied by the Germanic and Slavic Languages Department. An extensive renovation in the late 1990s restored many of the building's historical architectural features. Among previous notable occupants of Meigs Hall is former Georgia governor Zell Miller, who held a faculty position in the Institute of Higher Education for a year before being appointed to the U.S. Senate in 2000 to replace the deceased senator Paul Coverdell.

Motto and Seal

Early, sketchy records suggest that a UGA motto and seal were created chiefly by Josiah Meigs around 1801. The motto as it reads today—"To teach, to serve and to inquire into the nature of things"—captures the institution's three purposes: teaching, research, and public service. But the original Latin version—*"Et docere et rerum exquirere causas"*—translates as "To teach and to inquire into the nature [or cause] of things." The words "to serve" were added to the English version around 1990 during a university self-study for reaccreditation. The original Latin version has not been revised to include "service."

A university seal appearing on the first diplomas presented in 1804 was a simple circle around the words *"Universitas Georgiae Sigillum 1801"* (Seal of the University of Georgia 1801) and the Latin words of the motto. The current version of the seal, with an image of the Arch and the date 1785, was first used on diplomas in 1897. UGA's seal is modeled on the Great Seal of the State of Georgia. The Arch represents the state constitution; its three pillars represent the legislative, judicial, and executive branches of government, which underpin the constitution, whose principles are "Wisdom, Justice, Moderation"—the state motto. A small soldier under the Arch symbolizes the military's role in defending the constitution.

Moore College

BUILT: 1874 | NAMED FOR: Richard Moore, mayor of Athens | CURRENT USE: UGA's Honors Program | BUILDING 0025

Severe money shortages plagued the university after the Civil War, and this is the only existing building erected between the end of the war and the start of the twentieth century. Moore College was built to house the College of Agriculture and Mechanic Arts (A&M), which was started in 1872 with federal Morrill Act funds. Though technically part of the university, the A&M college operated as a separate entity. As its enrollment grew, Mayor Richard Moore of Athens, realizing the college's financial importance to the city, persuaded the city fathers to give the university $23,500 for construction of a larger home for the college. The building was sited in an undeveloped area west of the campus and was designed with its front facing town instead of the main campus in order to emphasize that the A&M college did not consider itself part of the university. It was named Moore College, instead of Moore Hall, to further underscore its independence. But its defiant placement served to open the way for eventual expansion of the campus to the west.

Designed by Leon Henri Charbonnier, a native of France who taught mathematics and engineering for almost forty years, Moore College is the only example of the French Second Empire architectural style on the UGA campus or anywhere in Georgia north of Macon. The original brick exterior was later covered by white stucco. Its features include a mansard roof with dormer windows and massive, solid pine entrance doors with beautiful molding detail. The building has housed the departments of physics, chemistry, engineering, and geography. In the late 1950s, it became the home of language departments, which remained there until an extensive renovation began in 1999. The work restored historical features and reconfigured the interior to add computer labs, computer-accessible classrooms, and a library for the Honors Program, which moved into the building in 2001.

Bernard Ramsey Sculpture

The sculpture in front of Moore College is of Bernard B. Ramsey, whose gifts to UGA, totaling some $44 million, made him the most generous benefactor in UGA history. A native of Macon, Georgia, Ramsey graduated from the university in 1937 with a business degree and enjoyed a successful career with Merrill Lynch & Co. in New York City, retiring as the firm's senior vice president. Ramsey attributed his business success to his student experiences as an ROTC cadet colonel, fraternity president, and business manager of the *Pandora* yearbook. He believed education is the foundation of a strong society, and said of his financial contributions to his alma mater: "I want a better student so we can build a better university, and I want a better university so we can build a better world." Much of his financial support was targeted toward encouraging student academic achievement through the Honors Program. His $18.8 million bequest for the Foundation Fellows scholarship program was the largest single gift ever made to the university. He earlier had donated more than $7.5 million to the Fellows program and other academic scholarships—an unsurpassed level of support for student scholarships. He also provided $2.5 million to endow the upkeep and operations of the student physical activities center, which is named for Ramsey and his first wife, Eugenia. His gifts to the Terry College of Business established an endowed professorship, created a center for the study of private enterprise, and funded an auditorium in the college's student center. He also endowed Eminent Scholar professorships in biology and microbial

Honors Program

For high school seniors trying to choose between attending a prestigious research university with leading scholars and outstanding scientific and academic resources, or an elite liberal arts college with small classes and personalized attention from professors, UGA offers a perfect solution—the Honors Program. Started in 1960, the program is one of the oldest and largest in the nation for academically advanced students. About 10 percent of each year's freshmen are admitted into the program, which maintains an annual enrollment of about 2,300. Honors faculty, chosen for their superior classroom skills and commitment to undergraduate instruction, teach classes that average seventeen students, hold book discussions in their homes, and gather with students over lunch to talk about their scholarly work. Honors students conduct frontline research projects under the guidance of a seasoned faculty mentor through the program's Center for Undergraduate Research Opportunities. A summer internship program sends honors students to Washington, D.C., New York City, and Savannah to work in congressional offices, government agencies, think tanks, law firms, and nonprofit organizations, while the Honors International Scholars Program enables students to work, study, and serve in countries around the world. A select few honors students are chosen for the Foundation Fellows Program, the university's premier undergraduate scholarship. In addition to covering most costs of attending UGA and offering small, accelerated classes taught by top senior professors, the Foundation Fellowship provides many specialized learning opportunities, including grants for travel in the United States and abroad for study and research; internships and participation in professional academic and scientific meetings; attendance at cultural events and dinner seminars with faculty members; meetings with leading scholars, dignitaries, and other notable visitors to campus; and a personal mentoring relationship with a faculty member. About 250 first-year honors students live in Myers Hall on South Campus, the designated magnet learning community for honors students, which includes a satellite advising office.

physiology, funded a concert hall in the Performing Arts Center, and helped fund the construction of Butts-Mehre Heritage Hall. Ramsey, who died in 1996, received the Terry College's Distinguished Alumnus Award and the university's Alumni Merit Award. His second wife, Doris, maintained his commitment to academic excellence and received the Blue Key Award and Friend of the University Award.

Candler Hall

BUILT: 1901 | NAMED FOR: Allen D. Candler, Georgia governor, 1898–1902 | CURRENT USE: School of Public and International Affairs | BUILDING 0031

Built in the showy Beaux-Arts style of architecture, Candler was nicknamed by students "Buckingham Palace" because of its resemblance to the home of the British royal family. Governor Allen Candler led efforts to persuade the General Assembly to provide funding for the building, which originally was

a men's residence hall. From 1942 to 1945, Candler housed cadets in the U.S. Navy's preflight training school. Later it was turned into an office building, converted back into a residence hall for women, and then reconfigured for classrooms and administrative offices. An extensive renovation begun in 2002 reversed many of the changes to the building's interior, including restoration of two staircases near the building's twin front entrances that had been demolished and rebuilt at the back of the main hall. The work raised ceilings to their original height, added hardwood floors, and allowed more light through the building's 125 windows. Other improvements included the addition of high-tech classrooms, a computer lab, and new mechanical, electrical, fire protection, and data systems. The School of Public and International Affairs (SPIA), created in 2001, moved into the building following the renovation.

Gilbert Hall

BUILT: 1942 | NAMED FOR: Judge Stirling Price Gilbert | CURRENT USE: Department of
Romance Languages, Institute for Women's Studies | BUILDING 0640

Several generations of students knew Gilbert Hall simply as "the infirmary,"
though its formal name was the Gilbert Memorial Infirmary. The infirmary
was a full-service medical facility with examination rooms, labs, an X-ray
room, a room for minor surgeries, an isolation room for contagious diseases,
and wards with private baths for extended care. An example of neoclassical
revival architecture, the building was constructed with money from the sale
of Coca-Cola stock given to the university by Stirling Price Gilbert, a justice
of the Georgia Supreme Court for almost twenty-five years. Gilbert made the
gift in memory of his father, Jasper N. Gilbert, a South Georgia doctor, and
his son, Francis Howard Gilbert, who graduated from UGA in 1927. The initial
funds were insufficient to construct the building as designed, and wings were
added to both sides in 1945. Immediately upon opening in 1943, the building
was pressed into use for the navy's preflight training school, and it did not
become a medical facility until after World War II. It housed the infirmary
until the new Student Health Center opened on East Campus in 1997, when
it was renamed Gilbert Hall and turned into space for the Department of
Romance Languages. The Institute for Women's Studies moved into the building in 2009.

Herty Field

BUILT: 1999 | NAMED FOR: Charles H. Herty, chemistry professor and coach of
UGA's first football team

For most of the university's first century, this placid green spot was a rocky,
weed-glutted hillside that marked the western edge of North Campus. After
the Civil War, military cadets drilled here and students held intramural athletic contests. In the 1880s, the baseball team played here. Charles Herty, who
was on the baseball team, graduated in 1886, earned a doctorate in chemistry
at Johns Hopkins University, and returned to UGA in 1890 to teach. A proponent of intercollegiate athletics, he organized a football squad and enlisted
students and townspeople to level and fill in the sloping area to create a football field. On January 30, 1892, Georgia beat Mercer College 50-0 in the first
intercollegiate football game played in the state. The area was named Herty
Field in 1896. When the baseball and football teams moved in 1911 to a new

UGA *Memory*

UGA holds a very special place in my heart. I
was a member of the UGA Redcoat Marching
Band, so I was on the field for many memorable
games, including the 2005 SEC Championship,
beating Tech all four years, and the Blackout
against Auburn. I was even given the opportunity to travel to China with the band. After
graduation, I left UGA for a job but stayed
close enough to Athens that I could visit often. My
boyfriend knew how much UGA meant to me,
so he planned his proposal accordingly. He
proposed on Herty Field. A few months later,
we had our engagement pictures taken at the
same spot. A year later, we went back to Herty
Field for our wedding photos. I plan on coming
back to dear Old Athens Town as often as I can
to surround myself in the many memories that
I have made.

Carmen Guisasola Andrews, Class of 2008

Georgia Colors:
Red and Black

Graduating classes in the nineteenth century customarily had a class song, a class cheer, and class colors. In December 1891, a month before the football team played its first intercollegiate game, against Mercer, editors of a student literary publication named the *Georgia University Magazine* took the custom a step further. The magazine declared that the university's official colors would be "old gold, black and crimson," and the magazine cover featured those hues. But football coach Charles Herty didn't like gold, considering it too similar to yellow and suggestive of weakness. Herty organized the first Athletic Association, which petitioned university trustees to eliminate gold because the association "did not want any yellow in Georgia athletics." As athletics grew in popularity, so did red and black. The student newspaper adopted the name the *Red and Black*, and the phrase popped up in early twentieth-century pep songs, including one titled "She's the Daughter of the Red and Black." A composition from 1908 titled "The Red and Black March" by R. E. Haughey, the first director of the Redcoat Band, was lost for several decades before a university staff member found a copy online. On October 7, 2008, the Redcoat Band played the march during halftime of the Georgia-Vanderbilt homecoming game, giving the piece its first public performance in nearly a century.

athletic stadium near what is now Sanford Stadium, the field became a popular gathering place for students and a site for intramural games and military drills. In 1938 the area was paved over, and for sixty-one years was a parking lot accessed by a street named Herty Drive. When the university implemented an environmentally focused campus master plan in 1999, the first step was to close Herty Drive and convert the parking lot to its present park-like appearance, making it again a popular place for study, relaxation, and social activities. In 2001, Herty Field was the site of a campus candlelight vigil following the September 11 terrorist attacks, and in 2002 it became the first place on campus to be in a wireless Internet cloud.

Charles Herty, who served also as athletic director, was responsible for installing the first tennis courts on campus, building the first campus gymnasium (in the basement of Old College), and helping create the Southern Intercollegiate Athletic Association to regulate college sports. He left UGA in 1902 and became a prominent chemical scientist whose research was instrumental in creating Georgia's pulp and paper industry.

Caldwell Hall

BUILT: 1981 | NAMED FOR: Harmon W. Caldwell, UGA president, 1935–48 | CURRENT USE: Terry College of Business, Department of Communication Studies | BUILDING 0046

When they opened in 1981, Caldwell Hall and the adjacent law library were the first major new construction projects on North Campus in almost thirty years. Some feared that seven-story Caldwell Hall would mar the historic character of North Campus, but it blended well with its surroundings and won architectural awards. In addition to general classrooms, the building was home to the College of Environment and Design until 2012, when the college moved to the renovated Visual Arts Building on Jackson Street.

Harmon Caldwell graduated from UGA in 1919, joined the School of Law faculty in 1929, and served as law school dean for two years before being named university president in 1935 at the age of thirty-six. During his tenure, the PWA buildings were constructed; more than one hundred new faculty members were added; the College of Veterinary Medicine and the *Georgia Review* were established; and the University of Georgia Foundation was created. In 1948, Caldwell became chancellor of the University System of Georgia and held the post until retiring in 1964.

Denmark Hall

BUILT: 1901 | NAMED FOR: Brantley A. Denmark, leader of the first alumni
fund-raising drive | CURRENT USE: graduate programs of the College of Environment
and Design | BUILDING 0044

This building was erected as the campus dining hall, and students called it
the "beanery," an uncomplimentary reference to the quality of food it served.
When the dining hall was moved in 1956, most of the building was con-
verted into classroom, studio, and office space for the Landscape Architecture
Department. A small luncheonette called the Co-op, relocated from New
College in the early 1950s, remained in the basement for a number of years.

Brantley Denmark, Class of 1871, was a prominent Savannah banker and a
university trustee. In 1897, the Alumni Society chose him to lead the university's first organized fund-raising drive. The effort brought in $40,000 for an
endowment that later was used to begin construction of the War Memorial
Hall (now called Memorial Hall). When Denmark died in 1901, this building was named for him. The metal sculpture in front of the main entrance,
titled *Field Cell*, was created by Jack Kehoe, a UGA art professor, and presented
to Hubert Owens, the founder of the landscape architecture program, on his
retirement in 1973.

Brooks Hall

BUILT: 1928 | NAMED FOR: Robert Preston Brooks, dean of the School of Commerce |
CURRENT USE: Terry College of Business | BUILDING 0055

Construction of this large neoclassical building, designed by the noted
Georgia architect Neel Reid, was paid for with $215,000 from an alumni fund-
raising drive conducted after World War I. For many years the north side of
the building was occupied by the School of Commerce, the south side was
home to the Henry W. Grady School of Journalism, and the structure was
known as the C-J Building. When the journalism school moved to new quarters in 1968, the business school expanded into the entire building. It was
extensively renovated and enlarged in 1972, and today includes a three-hun-
dred-seat auditorium, offices for more than 260 faculty and staff, and facilities for six specialized research centers, including studies in private enterprise,
economic growth, marketing, and nonprofit management. On the walls of the
first-floor hallway are four huge frescos painted by Jean Charlot, a visiting artist, between September 1943 and February 1944. Commissioned by the *Atlanta*

Journal newspaper for the journalism school, the paintings are Charlot's
impression of four important moments in communication history. On August
15, 1995, a spark from a workman's welding torch ignited a fire that severely
damaged the roof and top floors of Brooks Hall. No one was injured, but valuable equipment, furnishings, books, and research documents were destroyed.
One hundred firefighters poured more than 1.5 million gallons on the blaze,
which burned for six hours. Following $9 million in repairs and restoration,
the building reopened in January 1997.

The building was named in 1974 for Robert P. Brooks, a 1904 graduate who
was UGA's first Rhodes scholar. UGA established the School of Commerce in 1912,
becoming the first southern university, and one of the first in the nation, to create a business school. Brooks became dean in 1920, and during his twenty-five-
year tenure the school grew into the College of Business Administration. He
also served as dean of faculties, was a leader in the campaign that raised money
for this building, and was editor of the first alumni magazine. After retiring in
1952, he wrote a history of the university under its first sixteen presidents.

In 1991, the College of Business Administration was named in honor of
Herman Terry, a 1939 graduate of the commerce school, and his wife, Mary
Virginia Terry. The Terrys were major financial supporters of the college,
endowing faculty chairs, student scholarships, research programs, and facility upgrades. Herman Terry, who died in 1998, was a trustee of the UGA
Foundation and received the college's Distinguished Alumni Award. The university presented Mary Virginia Terry an honorary doctoral degree in 2009.

Sanford Hall

BUILT: 1997 | NAMED FOR: the family of Charles S. Sanford Jr. and his wife, Mary | CURRENT USE: Terry College of Business | BUILDING 0058

Charles Sanford Jr., retired board chairman and chief executive officer of Bankers Trust New York Corp., made the lead gift and chaired a campaign that raised $6.7 million from 1,200 donors to build Sanford Hall. A 1958 UGA graduate, Sanford has family ties to the university dating back to an ancestor who graduated in 1835. His grandfather, Steadman Sanford, was president of the university and chancellor of the University System of Georgia. His father, Charles S. Sanford Sr., Class of 1921, was a banker and civic leader in Savannah. His wife, the former Mary McRitchie, is a 1959 graduate.

Sanford Hall, encompassing thirty-eight thousand square feet, features advanced technology for business education. Its fifteen classrooms, ranging in size from a 330-seat auditorium to small seminar rooms, have a total of 900 seats, each with computer network connection and Internet access. About ninety desks are equipped with computers. There are video/data projectors, 3-D overhead projectors, and video and computer displays in some classrooms. The building includes a student advising center and a student lounge.

Founders Memorial Garden

BUILT: 1946 | NAMED FOR: the founders of the first garden club in the United States

This tranquil, meticulously groomed garden, listed on the National Register of Historic Places, honors the twelve Athens women who in 1891 founded the Ladies Garden Club of Athens, the first garden club in the United States. Delegates to the convention of the Garden Club of Georgia in 1936 voted to help fund the garden. It was designed by Hubert B. Owens, the head of the Landscape Architecture Department, which also provided funding. Work began in 1939 and was completed in 1946. The 2.5-acre garden was built around the Federal-style Lumpkin House, constructed in 1857 as the second faculty residence and used over the years for a variety of purposes, including classrooms, offices, a residence for students and faculty members, and the home of Phi Mu, the first social sorority at UGA. From 1963 to 1998, the Lumpkin House served as state headquarters of the Garden Club of Georgia, and it is now a museum house with period furnishings. A favorite spot for a relaxing outdoor lunch, a quick work break, or a quiet stroll, Founders Memorial Garden has several sections, including an open lawn with flagstone walks, slate walls, and a small fountain; a boxwood garden with boxwoods in the shape of four Georgia plants: a Cherokee rose, a peach, a watermelon, and a cotton boll; a perennial garden enclosed by serpentine walls with an arbor; a camellia walk; and the Living Memorial and Arboretum, which honors members of the armed forces. A number of plants in the garden, such as camellias, azaleas, and boxwoods, are commonly considered native to the southern United States but actually came originally from Japan and China. The garden is open daily during daylight hours, and admission is free.

Morris Hall

BUILT: 1957 | NAMED FOR: Sylvanus Morris, first dean of the School of Law, and his brother, John Morris, a professor of German | CURRENT USE: Student residence hall | BUILDING 2204

Morris Hall opened on January 1, 1958, as a residence hall for male law students and graduate students. Seventy-five rooms accommodated one hundred students, and the building had its own library. In 1973, it was used as a test site for twenty-four-hour student visitations, but women were not allowed to live here until 2001. Originally called the Law-Graduate Dormitory, it was named in 1963 for Sylvanus and John Morris, whose father, Charles Morris, was an English language and literature professor at UGA. Sylvanus earned a master's degree from the university in 1874 and a law degree in 1877 and joined the law faculty in 1893. As the school's first dean (from 1900), he is credited with turning what was essentially a small law-tutoring business into a comprehensive law school. He served as dean until 1927. John graduated from Randolph-Macon College in Virginia, earned a law degree at UGA in 1885, and after practicing law briefly in Alabama did postgraduate work at the University of Berlin. In 1893, he joined the faculty at UGA, where he taught German for fifty-two years.

If Joe Brown Could Talk . . .

All residence halls harbor stories about the playful, creative, and sometimes mischievous young people who live in them. But few dorms could tell tales more outrageous or more tragic than Joe Brown. One night soon after the building opened, a group of residents borrowed a van and drove to a private zoo in Atlanta. One of the zoo's occupants was an old, nearly toothless, and very docile lion. The young men enticed it into the van, brought it to Joe Brown Hall, and quietly led it into a room where several residents were sleeping. One of the pranksters kicked the lion, causing it to emit a ferocious roar, which awoke the sleeping students and sent them leaping out of windows. The lion then climbed on a bed and went to sleep. Police notified its owners, who returned the beast to its home no worse for the experience. Except for a student who suffered a sprained ankle from jumping out the window, and a bed that had a peculiar odor, the trick caused no lasting harm—except to the pranksters, who were all expelled. A more tragic event occurred in Joe Brown Hall in the early 1970s when a student committed suicide there during Christmas break. His body was not discovered for several days, and workmen were unable to thoroughly fumigate the room, which was at the top of a staircase. They sealed the room off, and as a result the set of stairs led to a wall. Around 2007, the Department of Germanic and Slavic Languages hung a large vertical photograph on the wall at the top of the stairs. The photograph, which depicts a doorway, from a distance gives the illusion that the stairs lead into a hallway. The photograph is actually a reproduction of a painting of the entrance into the apartment of the German writer Johann Wolfgang von Goethe.

Joe Brown Hall

BUILT: 1932 | NAMED FOR: Joseph E. Brown, Georgia governor, 1857–65 | CURRENT USE: Departments of Comparative Literature and Germanic and Slavic languages | BUILDING 0250

This Colonial Revival–style building has an unusual architectural feature: the front entrance, with a portico featuring Doric columns, is reproduced in a smaller version as a rear entrance. Originally opened as a residence hall for male students, the building housed navy cadets at the preflight training school during World War II and was again a dormitory after the war. It was converted into offices and classrooms for the Music Department before its current occupants moved in.

Joseph Brown, Georgia's governor during the Civil War, graduated from Yale Law School, but his sons attended UGA. He was a generous benefactor of the university, donating $50,000 in 1882 in honor of his son Charles, who died the year before. After his term as governor ended, Brown was appointed chief justice of the Georgia Supreme Court and served in the U.S. Senate from 1880 to 1891.

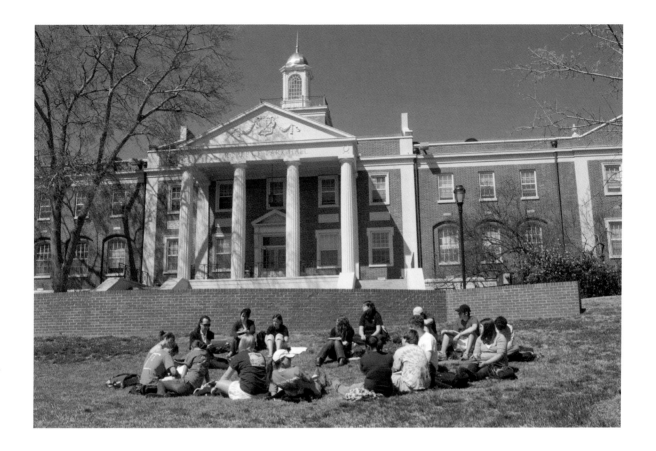

Park Hall

BUILT: 1938 | NAMED FOR: Robert E. Park, head of English Department, 1900–1942 |
CURRENT USE: English Department, Classics Department | BUILDING 0056

Prominent features of this Colonial-style building are four handsome Doric
columns and an internally floodlit cupola that rises through the center of its
three stories. Light filtering through stained-glass windows further illumi-
nates the rotunda beneath the cupola. Built with PWA funds, the building at
one time housed the Physics Department but has for many years been home
of the English Department. It was enlarged with an annex in 1970. Robert
Park, who came to UGA from the University of Alabama, was one of the most
popular professors on campus until his death in 1942. His portrait hangs in
the main hallway.

Natasha Trethewey

Natasha Trethewey, who earned a degree in
English in 1989, won the Pulitzer Prize for
poetry in 2007 and in 2012 was named U.S.
poet laureate.

Tanner Building

BUILT: 1909 | NAMED FOR: Tanner Lumber Company | CURRENT USE: College of Environment and Design | BUILDING 0123

This building began as a 50-foot-by-150-foot wooden structure erected in the late 1880s or early 1890s as a warehouse for the Central of Georgia Railroad. The Carter-Moss Lumber Company bought the structure in 1896 and added this brick building in 1909 as the front of the business. The brothers Tom and Gus Dozier purchased the business in 1926 and operated it as the Dozier Company until an employee, Johnnie B. Tanner Sr., bought it in 1947, when it became the Tanner Lumber Company. Tanner and his eldest son, J. Bryson Tanner Jr., operated the company until the senior Tanner's death in 1995, by which time the building and the 1.3 acres it occupied were surrounded by UGA property. The university, which wanted the land for a parking deck, bought the building and land in 1996 for $800,000, with the understanding that the building would be preserved. In 1998, it underwent a $245,000 renovation to install air-conditioning and update its electrical, mechanical, and plumbing systems. The building housed programs of the Lamar Dodd School of Art until 2008, and is now used for studios and classrooms of the College of Environment and Design. Behind the building is the $10 million North Campus Parking Deck, with spaces for more than twelve hundred vehicles, which also opened in 1998.

Bishop House

BUILT: 1837 | NAMED FOR: Thomas Bishop, an Athens merchant and farmer | CURRENT USE: College of Environment and Design | BUILDING 0032

Though not part of the North Campus quads, Bishop House is among the oldest existing university structures. Thomas Bishop came to Athens from Massachusetts in 1835 and opened a grocery store. He bought several acres of land on Jackson Street from the university Trustees and built this house, which remained in the possession of his descendants for more than one hundred years. One of the earliest remaining examples of Greek Revival architecture in Athens, the house was part of a farm that included a carriage house and stables, barns, a smokehouse, and fields for growing corn and vegetables. It is believed to be one of the first in Athens with running water, and it was long noted for beautiful landscaping that included boxwood plantings, flowering shrubs, and giant shade trees. UGA bought the property in 1942, and the house has been remodeled several times. It has been used as a residence hall for students and faculty members, offices and studios for the Art Department, and home of the Classics Department. Repurposed yet again in 2012, it now houses the external affairs staff of the adjacent College of Environment and Design. Bishop House is listed on the National Register of Historic Places.

Jackson Street Building

BUILT: 1961 | CURRENT USE: College of Environment and Design | BUILDING 0040

This building stood in stark contrast to the traditional architecture of North Campus when it opened as the Visual Arts Building, home of the Department of Art. Designed by the Atlanta architect Joseph Amisano to symbolize the creative energy and artistic vision of the department and its guiding light, the legendary UGA artist and art professor Lamar Dodd, the modernist fifty-three-thousand-square-foot structure was derided as the "Ice Plant" for its glass walls, high vaulted ceilings, and geometric lines. But it won national awards for innovative design and served almost five decades as a training ground for thousands of aspiring artists, sculptors, designers, and teachers, many of

whose creations were displayed in the building's galleries and on its lawns. In 1996, the department became the Lamar Dodd School of Art, and in 2008 the school vacated the building for a new home on East Campus. The building served as transitional space until 2011, when a $9.9 million renovation—a model of environmentally sustainable design—converted it into the new home of the College of Environment and Design.

The building, on track for LEED (Leadership in Energy and Environmental Design) Gold certification, is the first on campus to have rooftop solar panels, which were installed on the south-facing slopes of the roof's skylights. The seventy-two photovoltaic panels capture enough sunlight to generate about thirty thousand kilowatt hours of electricity each year—sufficient to power up to ninety fluorescent-light fixtures—and will pay for themselves in fourteen years through lower electricity costs. The building's numerous glass windows were replaced with glass that transfers less heat but allows natural light to filter into spacious open studios. Highly efficient heating and cooling systems were installed, along with a twenty-five-thousand-gallon cistern that collects rain and condensate from the cooling system for reuse in mechanical systems and for toilet flushing. About 90 percent of the glass and other materials removed in the renovation were recycled.

In addition to studios, the building contains a large exhibit gallery, a computer classroom, two large lecture halls, a design library, and a critique corridor. The College of Environment and Design was created in 2001 from the former School of Environmental Design. The college's landscape architecture program is the largest and one of the best in the nation.

Old Athens Cemetery

UGA is one of only a handful of U.S. colleges and universities with a cemetery on its campus. Old Athens Cemetery, also known as Jackson Street Cemetery, is the resting place of some of Athens's earliest citizens. The property was part of the 633 acres that John Milledge donated to the university. The university unofficially gave it to the city of Athens in 1810, and it was the community's main burial ground until Oconee Hill Cemetery opened in 1856. Originally more than twice its current size, the cemetery was a common burial ground, meaning that people wishing to bury someone did not purchase a plot but simply picked out a location, arranged for burial, and maintained the grave. Some eight hundred burial sites are thought to be in the current two and a half acres, but many graves are unmarked and many more undiscovered. The oldest grave is dated 1814, and the last known burial was in 1898. Among the identified graves are those of Revolutionary War and Civil War veterans, UGA students, local merchants and ministers, children of UGA president Alonzo Church, the first wife of Georgia governor Charles McDonald, and UGA president Robert Finley, who died in 1817, just a few months into his term. Its ownership unclear, the cemetery fell into a state of neglect after it was closed, and several times it was threatened with removal. A private foundation rescued it in the 1980s and in 2004 deeded it to UGA, which began a preservation project to document, clean, and restore the site. Using a geographic information system and ground-penetrating radar, workers have located unmarked graves and long-buried headstones, in addition to repairing monuments and buttressing crumbling walls and fences. The cemetery earned a listing on the National Register of Historic Places in 2011.

Baldwin Hall

BUILT: 1938 | NAMED FOR: Abraham Baldwin, first president of UGA, 1785–1801 | CURRENT USE: Departments of Anthropology, Sociology, Political Science, and Public Administration and Policy | BUILDING 0050

Another of the buildings erected with PWA funds, Baldwin Hall originally was a practice school for the School of Education. During World War II, it was headquarters for the navy preflight training school, which added an annex at the back for a dining hall. It later housed biological sciences departments, and the College of Education occupied the building from 1962 until 1971. In front of the building are two granite boulders into which are carved shapes and designs. The origin, purpose and meaning of these stones and their markings, known as petroglyphs, are a mystery. Anthropologists say the symbols are similar to designs found on pottery in Georgia from 800 years ago and may have been carved by Native Americans. The carvings could tell a story or could be some sort of map or guide. The smaller stone was found in White County and donated to UGA by citizens of the county around 1939. An Athens resident, H. F. Vaughn, found the larger stone, which weighs more than three tons, on property he owned in Forsyth County; he donated it in 1963. It rested for years near what is now the Administration Building.

CHAPTER 3

Central Campus

CENTRAL CAMPUS is bounded by Baldwin Street on the north, East Campus Road on the east, Field Street on the south, and Lumpkin Street on the west.

Tucked between the larger North and South Campuses, the compact Central Campus historically has been the home of student activities at UGA. The site of the first major athletic venues and the first nonacademic building for students, this is where generations of students have gathered to socialize, eat, and play, and more recently to study. Fittingly dominated by spacious buildings designed to enhance the quality of the student experience, Central Campus is perpetually abuzz with the energy and high spirits of youth, serving as the center of campus life for students.

The 37 acres designated for the UGA campus in the original 633-acre land grant included what is now Central Campus. But for the university's first century, much of this area was rugged woodland that included a deep ravine bisected by a stream called Tanyard Branch. As officials planned the university's southward growth in the early twentieth century, this daunting landscape, along with a politically driven desire to create an agricultural college apart from the rest of the campus, was a major factor in a decision to erect the first permanent building south of Old College on the south side of the ravine. That building, Conner Hall, was opened in 1908 on what is now South Campus.

The Central Campus area began to develop two years later when work started on a building that would become Memorial Hall. Intended as a kind of student athletic center, it had a gymnasium and swimming pool by 1912, when construction stopped because of money shortages. When fully completed in 1925, it became the hub of student programs.

Several athletic facilities that no longer exist were on Central Campus. They include Sanford Field, a stadium for football and baseball that was built in 1911; Woodruff Hall, a wood-frame basketball gymnasium built in 1925 and demolished in 1967; and six tennis courts that were installed in the 1930s and remained until the mid-1960s. In the early 1940s, the navy built a track and a gymnasium for cadets in the preflight training school. The track was the home of the UGA track team until it was removed in the early 1980s to make way for the Tate Student Center. The gymnasium, named Stegeman Hall, had a swimming pool where the varsity swim team competed. The gym was also was a venue for concerts and for years was the site of class registration. The building was razed in 1995 and its name transferred to the coliseum.

One athletic venue does remain, and it is the most famous spot at UGA. Sanford Stadium has been seen by football fans throughout the United States on nationally televised Bulldog home games and by millions of soccer fans around the world who watched soccer competitions held during the 1996 Olympics. Since the opening football game in the stadium in 1929, when Georgia beat Yale 15–0, the Bulldogs have won more than three hundred home games, thanks to the feats of such stars as Heisman Trophy winners Frank Sinkwich and Herschel Walker. Filled most Saturdays to its capacity of nearly ninety-three thousand, Sanford Stadium is one of the ten largest collegiate stadiums in the country and widely regarded as one of the most beautiful.

Central Campus features a major academic building, the popular University Theatre, and two residence halls. But the lifeblood of this sector is the massive Zell Miller Learning Center and Dean Tate Student Center. The Miller Learning Center is equipped with some of the most advanced technology available for classroom instruction and student learning. The Tate Center offers a vast range of programs, activities, and services to engage, entertain, and involve students. These facilities are key components of a comprehensive program of student services that make UGA a national leader in meeting the needs of today's students.

BALDWIN STREET

Fine Arts
Building
0060

Military Science
Building
0061

Psychology-Journalism Building
0062 / 0064

HOOPER STREET

SANFORD DRIVE

Payne Hall
0270

Zell B. Miller Learning Center
0081

Milledge Hall
0271

UGA Bookstore
0671

Memorial Hall
0670

Reed Hall
0280

Dean Tate Student Center
0672

*Jim Gillis
Bridge*

Fine Arts Building

BUILT: 1941 | CURRENT USE: Department of Theatre and Film Studies,
University Theatre | BUILDING 0060

Hailed by the *Pandora* yearbook as "a great advance in the building of a greater
University," and praised by the university alumni magazine for equipment
"unequalled by any university in the South," the Fine Arts Building was a but-
ton-popping source of pride to a Depression-weary university when it opened
in 1941. A model of neoclassical revival architecture, the building featured an
ornate interior designed by the English architect Sir John Sloan, a giant mural
painted by the acclaimed artist Jean Charlot, and an eighteen-hundred-seat
theater with state-of-the-art furnishings and acoustics. The $450,000 struc-
ture—the last built at UGA with PWA funds—was the most expensive building ever constructed at the university and one of the largest, with a footprint
equal to a city block. So proud were officials that they staged a five-day dedication festival featuring a theatrical production, an opera, and an exhibition
of paintings from the Metropolitan Museum of Art. The building housed the
Department of Art on one side, with studios, galleries, and classrooms; the
Department of Music on the other side, with soundproof practice rooms and
a large band room; and in the middle the Department of Drama, with a large

proscenium-style theater that included a balcony, patron boxes, an orchestra pit, and a dramatic domed ceiling with a skylight. The building's lobby, patterned after the one in the Bank of England, featured marble Corinthian columns, mirrored walls, and a deep rose carpet. Above six tall Ionic columns at the building's entrance, Charlot's three-panel fresco incorporated classical Greek themes to pay tribute to art, music, and drama.

The building, and especially the elegant theater, quickly became the cultural hub for the university and community, hosting theatrical productions, art shows, music and dance concerts, and speeches by visiting celebrities. But heavy use took its toll, and over the years the building's glory faded. The Art Department moved to new quarters in 1961, and in 1976 the theater was turned into a then-trendy "black box" space, which required blackening the domed ceiling, erecting black walls to conceal handcrafted fixtures and tiles, and installing sound-muffling air handlers on the stage. The balcony was also removed, halving the seating capacity. In 1995, the Music Department moved out, leaving the building solely to the Theatre and Film Studies Department.

In 2009, the university breathed new life into Fine Arts with a $4.5 million renovation that reversed many of the unfortunate "black box" changes. The domed ceiling and elaborate décor were restored, more seats were added, the floor was reoriented to provide better views of the stage, and state-of-the-art lighting and sound were installed. Charlot's mural was refurbished for the first time in sixty-one years. In addition to the main theater, the building has two smaller theaters for less elaborate productions. In a manicured plaza behind the building is a large abstract granite sculpture created by Abbott Pattison, a Chicago sculptor who was a visiting art professor in the early 1950s.

Military Science Building

BUILT: 1931 | CURRENT USE: Army ROTC | BUILDING 0061

UGA began requiring students to take military training in the 1870s as part of its land-grant mandate. In the early twentieth century, the military department included a cavalry unit and a small marching band. The department became an army ROTC unit three years after President Woodrow Wilson created the ROTC program in 1916. This building, constructed in Colonial Revival style and paid for with $10,000 provided by the University Cooperative Association, was originally called the armory and has always housed army ROTC. In addition to offices and classrooms, it originally had a rifle range in

Academically Outstanding Students

Despite producing fifteen Rhodes scholars in the first seventy-five years of the twentieth century, UGA was not known for outstanding student academic quality. That began to change in the 1980s as the university's academic reputation climbed and classroom teaching received greater emphasis. Student quality took a huge leap with the introduction of Georgia's HOPE Scholarship in 1993. Created by Governor Zell Miller (with help from UGA president Charles Knapp), the lottery-funded HOPE paid tuition and other expenses for Georgia high school graduates with a grade point average of at least 3.0. Bright students who previously might have gone to a top university in another state realized they could get a first-rate education at UGA at far lower cost. Within a few years, average freshmen scores on the Scholastic Achievement Test (SAT) soared ninety points, ranking UGA among the fifteen comprehensive public universities with the highest SAT scores. Today about 97 percent of the in-state freshmen who enroll qualify for either the HOPE Scholarship or its companion, the Zell Miller Scholarship. Since 1993, more than 301,000 UGA students have received HOPE or Miller awards, worth a total of more than $1.3 billion. The influx of higher-caliber students has sharply escalated student quality but also tightened admission qualifications, turning UGA into a highly selective public university. UGA's top student scholars are on an academic par with students at the nation's leading universities, as evidenced by their success in winning more than one hundred prestigious national undergraduate scholarships and fellowships between 1996 and 2012. Those awards included an additional eight Rhodes Scholarships, giving UGA a total of twenty-three Rhodes scholars—more than any other college in Georgia.

the basement. During the Vietnam War, the building was the target of protests, including a failed attempt to set it afire. The adjacent plaza was donated by the Army ROTC Alumni Association and dedicated in 1990 to former cadets. A fifty-one-hundred-gallon underground cistern behind the building collects rainwater to irrigate the nearby Memorial Service Garden.

Zell B. Miller Learning Center

BUILT: 2003 | NAMED FOR: Zell Miller, Georgia governor (1991–99) and U.S. senator (2000–2005) | CURRENT USE: Classrooms and facilities to promote student learning | BUILDING 0081

Occupying a 6.5-acre footprint, this 259,625-square-foot building is the largest on Central Campus and probably the most heavily used by students. Built specifically to enhance undergraduate learning, the MLC, as it is known to students, places UGA in the forefront of modern instructional technology. The building, which is open until 2:00 a.m. Monday through Thursday, has twenty-six classrooms with a total of twenty-two hundred seats, each with laptop connectivity. Other equipment in classrooms includes data/video projectors and screens; VCR, DVD, and cable access; auxiliary inputs for other audiovisual devices; real-time and e-mail feedback capabilities; and high-resolution document cameras. Students can

use specialized labs for instruction in electronic research sources, information literacy skills, and software applications. An electronic library provides access to online journals and books, research databases, and electronic indexes. There are five hundred public-access computers, ninety-six study rooms for individual or group work, a reading room, and a coffee shop.

The building, originally called the Student Learning Center, was named in 2009 to recognize Zell Miller's sixty years of public service, including serving two terms as the state's seventy-ninth governor and a stint in the U.S. Senate. As governor, Miller—who holds bachelor's and master's degrees from UGA—created Georgia's HOPE Scholarship and authorized more than $1 billion in capital spending for the state's public colleges and universities. On the north side of the MLC is the Memorial Service Garden, opened in 2005 to honor UGA students, faculty members, staff members, and alumni who have died in the nation's wars. Inside the MLC is a Book of Remembrance that lists names of those who have died in combat, training, or public service since 1785 (http://servicememorial.libs.uga.edu).

UGA Bookstore

BUILT: 1968 | CURRENT USE: Campus source for all things Bulldog | BUILDING 0671

The bookstore offers students one-stop shopping for virtually all their nonfood needs, both in and out of the classroom. The store carries new and used textbooks—including digital textbooks—and supplementary materials for courses taught in UGA classrooms as well as a selection of books and magazines. The bookstore stocks Athens's largest selection of UGA-themed apparel for adults and children, along with a large array of other merchandise, including artwork and posters, furniture, housewares, pet supplies, sporting goods, jewelry, and novelties. The store sells computers, computer supplies and accessories, other electronics, medical apparel and supplies, toiletries and cosmetics, toys, and UGA souvenirs. The bookstore is open to the public.

UGA *Memory*

My fondest memories of UGA, by far, are of my time spent as coordinator for the Committee for Black Cultural Programs (CBCP). During my tenure, we sought to expose students to culturally diverse events that would also bring support from community outlets. In that vein, we established an annual community event—the Day of Soul Arts Festival and Concert—which featured local artists, a caricaturist, face painters, free food, a live DJ, and a celebrated musician. Other annual events showcased new mainstream talent, focused on the achievements of prominent African Americans, and allowed major authors to share their work.

We took every opportunity to partner with other University Union divisions to cosponsor movies, concerts, and other performing arts programs. I remember using this platform to provide student members the ability to promote, market, and present events with the guidance of an adviser.

Some of the celebrities we were fortunate enough to bring to campus were Spike Lee, Speech and Arrested Development, Zhane, Terry McMillan, Nikki Giovanni, KRS-One, Chris Rock, Chris Tucker, Tommy Davidson, Lavelle Crawford, Hamburger, Kimberly Aiken (Miss America), Susan Taylor (*Essence* magazine editor), and various gospel artists.

It was an exciting time. Thanks, UGA, for this phenomenal experience!

Neicy Wells, Class of 1996

Dean Tate Student Center

BUILT: 1983, with a major addition in 2009 | NAMED FOR: William Tate, long-time dean of men | CURRENT USE: Primary location for student programs, events, and organizations | BUILDING 0672

If there is a heart of the UGA campus, the Tate Center is it. Thousands of students stream to this building daily to relax, socialize, eat, play, and take care of the business of being a UGA student. The state legislature provided $5.4 million for the original 120,000-square-foot building after years of prodding by university officials and students for a facility to replace Memorial Hall as a base for student activities. Two decades later, that facility was also inadequate, and students voted to pay an additional fee to help finance a $51 million, 95,000-square-foot addition, including a 508-space parking deck. In addition to offices and meeting rooms for student organizations, the center includes a game room, a theater that shows first-run movies, studios for student-operated radio station WUOG, two dance rehearsal rooms, six restaurants and eateries operated by University Food Services, and three franchise food outlets. There are other amenities also: a sports lounge, a print and copy center, the student ID office, a passport office, and a voter registration site. A twelve-thousand-square-foot multipurpose space can accommodate up to sixteen hundred people for concerts and lectures. Other features include a small amphitheater with a projection system and a seventeen-foot screen, an elegant dining room, a large conference room, and many spacious lounge areas. The U.S. Green Building Council awarded the student center Gold LEED certification in recognition of environmental features including a green roof, a seventy-five-thousand-gallon cistern that catches rain and condensate water for reuse in irrigation and toilet flushing, an energy-saving mechanical system, and use of low-volatile-organic-compound materials to enhance air quality.

William Tate enrolled in UGA in 1920 and was associated with the university for sixty years as a student, teacher, and administrator. A walking encyclopedia of Georgia and university history, Tate is remembered by legions of alumni simply as Dean Tate, the title he earned by serving as dean of men from 1946 until his mandatory retirement in 1971. Legendary for his ability to remember students' names, he had a deserved reputation as a gruff and vigilant enforcer of the university's behavior rules. But Tate also quietly helped countless students in times of crisis and need, and played a crucial role in maintaining order and calm during such campus crises as integration, Vietnam War protests, and demonstrations against student conduct regulations. After retiring, he remained as an alumni liaison and goodwill ambassador for the university until his death in 1980.

Student Organizations

Going to classes and studying, hanging out with friends, attending sports events, and taking in local music make for full lives for most students. But for those with extra time on their hands, more than six hundred organizations offer ways to stay busy—and in many cases, to do something beneficial. To meet the interests and needs of students, UGA offers sports clubs, religious groups, organizations for international students, professional societies, groups that recognize academic achievement and leadership, social fraternities and sororities, philanthropic and charitable groups, community and public service clubs, political groups, and dozens of special-interest groups as diverse as the Aardvark Army, the Anti-Bullying Organization, the Jam Band Society, and Young Americans for Liberty. Many groups address societal problems such as hunger, homelessness, and poverty; others conduct blood drives, mentor children, and raise money for good causes. Examples include the student Relay for Life, which has raised more than $2.3 million for the American Cancer Society, and Dance Marathon, a twenty-four-hour dance fest that has generated more than $2 million for Children's Healthcare of Atlanta. In the unlikely event a student can't find anything of interest, the Center for Student Organizations, a part of the Division of Student Affairs, will be happy to help start a new group.

George Foster Peabody Awards

On the third floor of the Grady College of Journalism and Mass Communication is the Peabody Awards Suite, home of the Peabody Award. First presented in 1941, it is the oldest and one of the most prestigious honors in broadcasting. Recipients, chosen strictly on the basis of quality rather than commercial success, include some of the most famous programs and personalities in broadcasting as well as hundreds of local radio and television stations that have provided exemplary public service to their audiences. The award was created when the National Association of Broadcasters formed a committee in 1938 to recognize radio stations for excellence. UGA's School of Journalism agreed to sponsor the award and named it in honor of the UGA benefactor George Foster Peabody. CBS won the first award for radio, and the first television award was presented in 1947. Categories have been added for cable television, home-video release, CD-ROM, and the World Wide Web. More than a thousand entries are typically submitted for the annual judging. Winners are chosen by a panel of distinguished scholars, television critics, industry practitioners, and experts in culture and the arts. Virtually every entry that has been submitted is held in the Walter J. Brown Media Archives and Peabody Awards Collection, stored in UGA's Richard B. Russell Building Special Collections Libraries.

UGA Pulitzer Prize recipients

The Pulitzer Prize for newspaper reporting has been awarded to eight graduates of the Grady College of Journalism and Mass Communication either individually or as members of a newspaper staff.

Psychology-Journalism Building

BUILT: 1968 | CURRENT USE: Department of Psychology (east side), Henry W. Grady College of Journalism and Mass Communication (west side) | BUILDINGS 0062/0064

For many years the university's tennis courts and a gymnasium named Woodruff Hall occupied the site where this sprawling structure sits. The area was cleared in 1967 to make way for the largest and most expensive ($6.1 million) single academic structure erected at UGA during the 1960s. Psychology is one of the most popular undergraduate majors, and the department, established in 1921, is one of the largest in the Franklin College of Arts and Sciences. In addition to classrooms and offices, the psychology building contains labs and other facilities for research, along with a clinic that provides psychological services to the Athens community.

The journalism school, named for the famed *Atlanta Constitution* editor and "Voice of the New South," was established in 1916 and is one of the nation's oldest and most distinguished communications programs. The journalism building houses specialized facilities to train students in such skills as audio and television production, newspaper and magazine production, advertising, public relations, graphics, and media management. The building also houses the studios of WUGA-TV, the university's public television station. The P-J complex includes two large multiuse auditoriums. On the ground level between the psychology and journalism buildings is Instructional Plaza, where the Willson Center for Humanities and Arts and the offices of other specialized programs are located.

Red and Black

Many national communications leaders, including Pulitzer Prize–winning writers, top advertising and public relations professionals, and executives of major media corporations, got their start by writing stories, selling ads, and laying out pages for the *Red and Black*. Born in a frenzy of athletics boosterism, the paper became a vehicle for students to share news (and sometimes gossip), voice opinions, irritate administrators, and push for improvements in student life. It has also been a training ground to teach generations of journalists the basics of writing, editing, design, and newspaper production.

Members of the Demosthenian and Phi Kappa literary societies published the first *Red and Black* on November 24th, 1893, working out of space in what is now the Academic Building. The editors proclaimed the paper's purpose to be "the general advancement of the University, as a whole, the interests of the Faculty and students." But the first issue was devoted almost entirely to the football team's recent loss to Vanderbilt, and for much of its early life the paper was the official organ of the Athletic Department. In 1928, the School of Journalism took it on as a laboratory class. Supported by advertising and subsidized by student fees, the paper was housed first in the basement of the Commerce-Journalism Building (now Brooks Hall) and after 1968 in the journalism building. In 1980, following a series of contentious disagreements, the university and the *Red and Black* agreed to sever ties. The paper moved off

campus and became an independent entity financed by advertising and published by a nonprofit corporation.

The paper was a weekly tabloid until 1963, when it began publishing twice weekly. The format was enlarged to a broadsheet in 1969, and in 1991 it began publishing Monday through Friday. In 2011, the paper went entirely online except for a printed edition on Thursdays. The *Red and Black* has staunchly championed the use of open-record and freedom-of-information laws, sometimes resorting to legal action. Its editors have never shied away from criticizing fellow students, faculty, administrators, and politicians, who in turn sometimes fault the paper for amateurish journalism. Infrequent attempts to impose control over reporting or quell the paper's editorial voice have resulted in well-publicized staff resignations that usually draw quick support for the student journalists. In 1993, a state historical marker commemorating the paper's centennial was installed on the west side of Academic Building.

UGA *Memory*

Although there were many great times at UGA, to the surprise of anyone who knows me, this memory is not about football or the escapades at the Sigma Nu house, but takes place in a classroom.

A major part of the grade in experimental psychology depended upon students' ability to educate a white mouse. That is, each student trained his little creature to execute certain required elements (similar to an Olympic gymnast, I suppose you could say) according to a schedule, and our grades depended on how well the mouse performed. Well, I can say with absolute certainty that I had the dumbest rat in Athens, because I flunked the course. Now you can say that was due in large part to my own ineptitude, and I would initially be tempted to agree; HOWEVER, as a psych major, I was required to retake the class, and did so the next quarter: and to the astonishment of many, excelled with an A (credit goes here to the smartest, most beautiful rat in Athens!). If I had continued on with the original animal, I definitely would have had to change my major, and probably never graduated. Go Dawgs! (and smart mice).

Tom Luther, Class of 1970

Memorial Hall

BUILT: 1925 | NAMED FOR: Alumni who died in World War I | CURRENT USE: Office of the Vice President for Student Affairs, Department of Intercultural Affairs, Office of Judicial Programs, academic advising units of the College of Arts and Sciences | BUILDING 0670

Memorial Hall may be one of the most versatile buildings on campus, having served many functions over some ninety years. In the late 1890s, a group of alumni concerned about the university's poor financial status raised about $40,000, which was set aside in an endowment when the leader of the drive died. Several years later, the University Alumni Society and the Athens YMCA joined to build a YMCA building on campus, but the plan fell apart over disagreements about the site. The YMCA gave the alumni about $6,000 it had collected for the project. With that money, plus the $40,000 in the endowment and a $15,000 gift from George Foster Peabody, the university in 1910 started work on a building that was intended to be a kind of student athletic center. But construction stopped two years later when money ran out, and the building sat unfinished until after World War I.

In 1922, the Alumni Society launched the university's first large-scale fundraising drive, called the War Memorial Fund, which eventually brought in more than $800,000. Some of the money funded completion of this building, which was named War Memorial Hall in honor of forty-seven students and alumni who died in World War I. Their names are engraved on a bronze plaque encircling the top of the lobby rotunda. The inscription, composed by university chancellor David Barrow, reads: "In loyal love we set apart this house, a memorial to those lovers of peace who took arms, left home and dear ones, and gave life that all men might be free." Eventually, the word "war" was dropped from the name, and Memorial Hall evolved into a hub for student activities.

The building originally had a swimming pool, gymnasium, and dressing rooms used by the Athletic Department. Over the years, it has housed a student dining hall, the University Bookstore, a library, the student radio station, student lounges, offices for student organizations, athletic offices, a faculty dining room, and administrative offices of both the College of Arts and Sciences and the vice president for student affairs. The navy enlarged Memorial Hall for its preflight training school, and the building served for a while as a residence for international students. During the university's bicentennial, it was a museum showcasing memorabilia from UGA's first two hundred years. A renovation of the second, third, and fourth floors in 2012

restored some historical features, including original light fixtures, wood paneling, and wood floors. Memorial Ballroom has long been a venue for dances, parties, receptions, and other social events. For more than forty years, the ballroom has been the site of the weekly International Coffee Hour, where UGA students from around the world gather to eat and socialize. The coffee hour is one of the longest-running programs of its kind in the country.

No history of UGA would be complete without mention of the legendary dean of men. My path first crossed with "Wild Bill" when, as a young freshman in 1967, I committed an unpardonable sin—pulling a fire alarm in Payne Hall on a wicked cold night. Bottom line, my dad (away on business in Detroit) and Dean Tate had a telephone conversation resulting in my being remanded to Armstrong State College in my hometown of Savannah for a quarter—kicked out of Georgia!

I did return, and on my second UGA graduation (master's degree), Dean Tate greeted my dad and my beaming family with the following: "Well, we finally got him through it, didn't we?" What a memory! Thanks Dean Tate for your wisdom and confidence.

Robert L. (Bob) Lowe Jr., Class of 1972; MPA, 1974

Milledge Hall

BUILT: 1925 | NAMED FOR: John Milledge, Georgia governor, 1802–6; donor of land for UGA's campus | CURRENT USE: Division of Academic Enhancement and Academic Resource Center | BUILDING 0271

This Colonial Revival structure, a gift of Clarke County through the post–World War I War Memorial Fund, was built as a residence hall for men. Wings financed by PWA funds in 1938 enlarged it into a residence hall for 182 male law students and graduate students and added a small law library. (Morris Hall later took over these functions from Milledge Hall.) It eventually became a general male residence hall. In 1992, it was renovated into office space for the Division of Academic Enhancement, which provides services to support student academic achievement, including specialized courses, tutoring, and workshops.

John Milledge, a Revolutionary War hero, paid a local entrepreneur, Daniel Easley, $4,000 for 633 acres and immediately donated the land for the original UGA campus. The next year, Milledge was elected governor of Georgia.

Payne Hall

BUILT: 1940 | NAMED FOR: William Oscar Payne, history professor and chairman of athletics | CURRENT USE: Student residence hall | BUILDING 0270

Partially funded with a PWA grant, Payne Hall was built for $92,000. Modeled after Milledge Hall and originally called "Milledge Annex," it was intended to be a residence hall for one hundred male students. But early on it became a dorm for football players and later other male athletes (among its residents was Frank Sinkwich, winner of the Heisman Trophy in 1942). After housing cadets of the navy preflight training school (1943–45), it was enlarged by the addition of two wings in 1951. It was named in 1953 in honor of William Payne, who earned bachelor's and master's degrees at UGA and in 1901 became a tutor in the Department of History and Political Science, where he spent his entire academic career. Chancellor S. V. Sanford appointed Payne the faculty chairman of athletics, a position he held for many years.

Reed Hall

BUILT: 1952 | NAMED FOR: Thomas W. Reed, longtime university registrar and historian | CURRENT USE: Student residence hall | BUILDING 0280

Reed Hall is one of two early-1950s buildings that were erected adjacent to existing buildings in order to form residence-hall quadrangles (Myers Hall on South Campus was the other), a popular concept for student housing at the time. Reed accommodated five hundred men and for many years was reserved for freshmen. Residents earned the nickname "student pigeons" for their habit of perching on the roof to watch football games in Sanford Stadium before a

Commencement Procession

UGA commencement for undergraduates is held in Sanford Stadium, and the ceremony for graduate students is in Stegeman Coliseum. Both ceremonies begin with a formal academic procession of black-robed university officials, dignitaries, faculty members, and graduating students. At the head of the procession, stiffly attired in a planter's hat, black morning coat, ascot, and red cummerbund, and holding aloft a gleaming sword, is the sheriff of Clarke County. The tradition of the sheriff leading the graduation party dates to UGA's first commencement, in 1804, when the sheriff of what was then Jackson County escorted President Josiah Meigs and nine young men to a brush arbor erected especially for the ceremony. A long-standing myth held that the sheriff's presence was meant to protect the graduating party from Indians. Creeks and Cherokees did live in the area, but were generally on friendly terms with whites and posed little danger. The sheriff's role in leading the graduation procession was ceremonial, likely a carryover from the prominent position the high sheriff held in English counties.

stadium enlargement blocked the view. In 1962, a year after the university was integrated, Harold Black, a freshman from Atlanta, moved into Reed, becoming the first African American male student to live in a residence hall. The building originally was designed in the customary style of the day, a barracks-type arrangement with small rooms on each side of long hallways and communal bathrooms. After years of wear, the building underwent a $10.4 million renovation in the late 1990s that reconfigured the interior into single rooms or suites for 296 students. The work added kitchens and study lounges and gave each room free Internet access.

Thomas Reed, affectionately known as "Uncle Tom," was a UGA mainstay for decades. After earning an undergraduate degree in 1888 and a law degree the next year, he practiced law and was editor of the *Athens Banner-Herald* before joining UGA in 1909 as secretary-treasurer of the board of trustees, a position he held for twenty-three years. In addition, he served as registrar for thirty-five years, until his retirement in 1945. In the five years before his death, he compiled a massive informal history of the university that filled some two thousand typewritten pages. Though never published in print but available electronically, his work has been a valuable resource for researchers.

Jim Gillis Bridge

CONSTRUCTED: 1963 | NAMED FOR: James L. Gillis Sr., director of the Georgia State Highway Board

For many years, the main way that students traveled between North and South Campuses was by climbing up and down steep concrete steps into and out of the deep valley that separated the campuses. Making the trek in the ten minutes between class periods was nearly impossible for students who needed to schedule consecutive classes on the two campuses. The problem was finally solved when the state provided $255,000 for this bridge, which spans Tanyard Branch and connects the campuses (portions of the old steps remain on both sides of the main gate to Sanford Stadium). The bridge was also viewed as a symbol for tempering a civil but spirited rivalry that had long existed between the "old fogies" of North Campus, with its focus on the humanities and social sciences, and the "Cow College" on South Campus, with its agricultural tradition. The bridge is closed weekdays to motorized traffic except university buses and vehicles. Football fans jam the bridge before home games to cheer as the Redcoat Band ushers the Bulldogs under the bridge and into Sanford Stadium in the famous Dawg Walk.

Gillis, a native of Soperton, Georgia, served in the Georgia House of Representatives and Georgia Senate and was director of the State Highway Board through much of the 1950s and 1960s. He was instrumental in creating Georgia's modern system of roads and highways.

CHAPTER 4

South Campus

SOUTH CAMPUS is bounded on the north by Field Street, on the east by East Campus Road, on the west by Lumpkin Street, and on the south by Pinecrest Drive.

Opened early in the twentieth century as the home of the university's agricultural programs, South Campus is the largest of the five campus sectors, stretching more than a mile from north to south. The area nicknamed "Ag Hill" is still home to the College of Agricultural and Environmental Sciences, but also harbors world-class science and research facilities and is headquarters for UGA's far-flung public service and outreach enterprise. With a blend of architectural styles ranging from traditional to modern, South Campus has two of the university's tallest buildings and features a sweeping, finely manicured mall where there once was a street. All but two of the major South Campus buildings were constructed in the twentieth century, but several bear witness to landmark moments in UGA history. South Campus is also home of many of the university's outstanding athletic facilities.

The original university campus ended where a deep, wooded ravine cut through the area that is now Central Campus. The land south of the ravine was part of the original grant from John Milledge, but by 1900 most of it had been sold and then lay within the Athens town limits. Governor Wilson Lumpkin bought some of the land in 1835 as part of tract totaling nearly a thousand acres, on which he established his retirement farm. In 1844, he built a home that still stands as one of the first permanent structures in the area.

One of Chancellor Walter Hill's first goals upon taking office in 1899 was to expand the campus in order to provide new facilities and resources for agricultural education and outreach. Hill and his friend and adviser George Foster Peabody engaged the well-known landscape engineer Charles Leavitt Jr. to create a long-range master plan for campus development. A key part of the plan called for moving agricultural programs away from North Campus to the area near the Lumpkin property.

Peabody bought nearly four hundred acres of land, including the Lumpkin home, for $22,000 and donated it to the university. With help from other sources, including a $25,000 gift from the city of Athens, the university acquired an additional seventy-one acres. All that land became the home of the new College of Agriculture, which the legislature created in 1906 as a secondary part of the existing College of Agriculture and Mechanic Arts as a way to help the A&M college retain federal funding. A state representative named James J. Conner helped persuade the legislature to appropriate $100,000 for the new college, and in 1908 a large building named Agricultural Hall (later renamed Conner Hall) opened on a spot beside the Lumpkin house.

Facilities for the agricultural program, including barns, animal shelters, greenhouses, pastures, and cultivation fields, sprang up around Conner Hall. A second permanent building, Barrow Hall, opened in 1911, and a third building, Hardman Hall, opened in 1922. Ag Hill encompassed two hundred acres by 1922 and eight hundred by 1932.

In the early 1920s, the agriculture college opened a summer camp for boys and girls in the 4-H program. Located on the southernmost edge of the South Campus area, Camp Wilkins—named for the Athens banker John Wilkins, who helped fund it—had a small lake, a baseball diamond, tennis courts, trails, and a building with a dining hall and bedrooms. The camp was closed in the 1960s, and its facilities were removed to make way for other construction. Many other agricultural structures and spaces that have dotted South Campus, such as residences, shops, barns, poultry houses, veterinary labs, pastures, and cultivation fields, have vanished over the years.

The first women admitted as regular students in 1918 were enrolled in the agriculture college's home economics division, and the college constructed three buildings for them on South Campus: Soule Hall, which opened in 1920 as the first women's dormitory; a women's health and physical education building, erected in 1928; and Dawson Hall, which opened in 1932 for home economics classes.

Three of the buildings constructed on South Campus with PWA grants in the years before World War II were agricultural facilities—the Hoke Smith Building (1937), a dairy science building (now Environmental Health Sciences, 1939), and the Hoke Smith Annex (1940). Three other PWA buildings were residence halls—Mary Lyndon Hall (1936), Clark Howell Hall (1937), and Rutherford Hall (1939). Mary Lyndon and Rutherford were built perpendicular to Soule Hall, forming three sides of a square that was closed with construction of Myers Hall in 1952. The resulting quadrangle became a favorite place for student games and gatherings. Nine years later, Myers was in the national media spotlight as the site of a raucous demonstration against UGA's racial desegregation.

With the end of World War II, returning veterans, taking advantage of the popular GI Bill, flooded to UGA and sent enrollment soaring beyond eight thousand. To house the veterans, many of whom were married with children, the university hurriedly set up 100 trailers and 260 prefab housing units in an area on the edge of South Campus that came to be known as Trailertown. The community, which included nurseries, laundry units, a recreational hall, a post office, and a cannery, thrived until the early 1950s, when most of the veterans had graduated and enrollment fell.

Construction of the modernistic six-building Science Center in 1959–60 gave South Campus not only a new "look" but also a new identity as the emerging locus for scientific research. Large infusions of federal, state, and private research funds brought about the construction of additional science facilities and a science library and helped thrust UGA into the ranks of top U.S. research universities. Today some of the nation's most advanced research in such fields as genetics, infectious diseases, and animal health occurs in buildings on South Campus.

South Campus is also the birthplace and traditional hub of UGA's expansive network of public service and outreach programs. For many years the university mainly fulfilled its land-grant mandate for public service through an extension service and related efforts in the College of Agriculture aimed chiefly at farmers and rural families. In the early twentieth century, programs were started to help local governments around the state. The service mission received a huge boost with the opening in 1957 of the Georgia Center for Continuing Education, one of the largest university-based adult-education enterprises in the country. Today the university's public service reach extends to every part of the state—and far beyond, with programs to assist governments and citizens in other countries.

As part of its commitment to making the campus greener, the university dug up a street that cut through the heart of South Campus and replaced it with a graceful pedestrian mall. Newer buildings in the area have been equipped with the latest technology for energy and water conservation, recycling, and pollution control.

Though it retains its Ag Hill nickname, South Campus has evolved from its agricultural beginnings more than a century ago into a center for world-class scientific research and the home of a leading university public service program. The area will continue to change with the move of the College of Veterinary Medicine Teaching Hospital to a new off-campus site. What won't change is South Campus's unique and distinctive contributions to the university's climb to educational excellence.

Much of the southern part of South Campus is dominated by athletic venues, including Stegeman Coliseum, Foley Field, the Dan Magill Tennis Complex, Spec Towns Track, and Butts-Mehre Heritage Hall. Information on these and other athletic facilities is in chapter 7.

Clark Howell Hall
0290

Geography-
Geology
1002

Chemistry / Center
for Computational
Quantum Chemistry
1001

Physics
1003

SCIENCE CENTER

Lumpkin House
1012

Biological
Sciences
1000

Conner Hall
1011

CEDAR STREET

LUMPKIN STREET

Rutherford
Hall
1210

Dawson Hall /
Speirs Hall
1010

Poultry
Science
1013

Myers
Hall
1222

Barrow Hall
1021

Mary Lyndon
Hall
1221

Soule
Hall
1220

Science
Library
1621

Boyd
Graduate
Studies
Building
1023

Food
Science
1020

Treanor
House
1657

SANFORD DRIVE

R. CHAPPELLE MATTHEWS
PUBLIC SERVICE COMPLEX

Marine Sciences /
Dance Building
1030

Hardman
Hall
1031

Statistics / EITS /
Museum of Natural
History
1130

J. W. Fanning
Building
1675

Georgia Center
for Continuing
Education
Conference
Center and Hotel
1640

Snelling Hall
1643

Robert
Wilson
Pharmacy
Building
1041

Ecology
Building
1033

Hoke Smith
Building / Hoke
Smith Annex
1042

The Gardens
at Athens
1340

Forestry and
Natural Resources
Building
1040 / 1140 /
1044 / 1046

Fred C. Davison
Life Sciences
Complex
1057

College of Family
and Consumer
Sciences
McPhaul Center
1246–1249 / 1652

Pharmacy
South
1038

Environmental
Health Science
Building
1050

CARLTON STREET

D.W.
Brooks
Mall

Miller Plant
Sciences Building /
Alan Jaworski
Plant Science
Amphitheater
1061

Tucker
Hall
1250

Aderhold
Hall
1060

Paul Coverdell
Center for
Biomedical and
Health Sciences
1111

Veterinary Medicine
Building
1070

EAST CAMPUS ROAD

Driftmier
Engineering Center
1090

On the morning of February 27, 1970, with the end of the quarter near, I had just given my last speech in speech class in Park Hall and made my way to Stegeman Hall, past the Fine Arts Building, the campus police station, and the Dixie Redcoat band room, for a makeup day in my coed badminton class.

I played against the badminton coach and a brunette with whom I had briefly talked at the beginning of the quarter. I can still remember looking across the badminton net at her in her baggy gym shorts and captivating eyes, the brightly polished wooden floors of Stegeman Hall gleaming in the background. Afterward, we walked down the Stegeman parking lot, past the new bookstore, and up to the Bulldog Room for a Coke. We talked for more than an hour before I drove her back up the hill on Baxter Street to Creswell Hall.

Before she got out of the car, we had a date for that night. I went down Lumpkin and noticed that the leaves weren't out on the trees in the park between Clark Howell and Myers Halls across the street from Church and Boggs Halls, but spring had already hit Athens for me! We've been married for forty years, and we have yet to play badminton again.

Robert Agress, Class of 1972

Clark Howell Hall

BUILT: 1937 | NAMED FOR: Clark Howell, prominent editor and political figure in nineteenth-century Georgia | CURRENT USE: UGA Career Center | BUILDING 0290

Built at a cost of $35,000, including PWA funds, Clark Howell Hall was originally a dormitory for one hundred male students. The Colonial Revival–style building—the first steel-frame construction in the Southeast—has a small right wing and a left wing that is almost as long as the building's front façade. Men lived here from 1937 until 1958, when it became a women's dormitory. In 1977, it underwent an extensive renovation that reconfigured the interior for offices and added an elevator, central air and heating, and a new entrance. The Northeast Georgia Police Academy occupied the building for several years before the Career Center moved in.

Clark Howell graduated from UGA in 1883 and joined the *Atlanta Constitution*, where he succeeded Henry W. Grady as editor. He served in the Georgia legislature as Speaker of the House and president of the Senate. As a UGA trustee for thirty-one years, he led efforts to admit women to the university. Howell died in 1936, and this building was named for him the following year.

Science Center

Physics: BUILDING 1003 | Geography-Geology: BUILDING 1002 | Chemistry / Center for Computational Quantum Chemistry: BUILDING 1001 | Biological Sciences: BUILDING 1000 | Poultry Science: BUILDING 1013 | Food Science: BUILDING 1020

A long-range plan for campus growth created in 1953 envisioned a "science complex" along the curved slope of the hill south of Sanford Stadium. The development was proposed as a way to bolster the university's growing emphasis on scientific research by providing space and technology to replace overcrowded and outdated science facilities on North Campus. Though popular, the plan was delayed—largely because of its projected $12 million cost—until 1957, when the launch of *Sputnik* shook Americans' confidence in their scientific leadership and ignited a new emphasis on scientific research. Part of the State of Georgia's response was to create the Science Center, consisting of six buildings: Physics (1959), Food Science (1959), Geography-Geology (1960), Chemistry (1960), Biological Sciences (1960) and Poultry Science (1960). A Computational Quantum Chemistry building was added in 1997.

With their flat roofs, sleek lines, and unadorned façades, these modernistic structures contrasted sharply in architectural style with other campus

UV-B Monitoring Center

UGA scientists established the National UV-B Monitoring Center, the first center in the country to monitor changes in the level of ultraviolet light striking the earth.

Dr. Francis G. Slack

Dr. Francis G. Slack, Class of 1918, was on the research team that conducted experiments leading to the first documented and verified fission of uranium (splitting of the uranium atom). Slack was also part of the Manhattan Project, which developed the first atomic bomb in 1945. A colleague in this work, Eugene Booth, earned bachelor's (1932) and master's (1934) degrees from UGA.

UGA and the Poultry Industry

Tunnel ventilation and evaporative cooling systems for poultry houses developed at UGA are used worldwide and have saved the Georgia poultry industry millions of dollars.

buildings of the time and symbolically proclaimed UGA's advance into a new era of scientific exploration. Key science departments of the Franklin College of Arts and Sciences moved from the crowded North Campus to the Science Center, furthering the demarcation between North Campus as the traditional home of the humanities and social sciences and South Campus as the futuristic venue for scientific research. Atop the Physics Building is a telescope that often is open to the public for viewing the night sky. The Geography-Geology Building has displays of rocks, minerals, fossils, maps, and scientific instruments; it was the first building on campus with a "green roof" for growing flowers, vegetables, and shrubs. The building also has a giant geophysical globe and a three-ton rock formed from sediment deposited when the Appalachian Mountains emerged more than 400 million years ago. The

Chemistry Building contains a display of instruments used over the years to measure the weight of chemicals. The Food Sciences Building has an exhibit on the development of techniques for food handling and preservation.

Dawson Hall / Speirs Hall

BUILT: 1932 | NAMED FOR: William T. Dawson, a major donor to the College of Agriculture; Mary Speirs, dean of the School of Home Economics, 1954–71 | CURRENT USE: College of Family and Consumer Sciences | BUILDING 1010

When women were admitted as regular students in 1918, the College of Agriculture and Mechanic Arts created a Division of Home Economics that would be responsible for teaching courses in such areas as nutrition and food preparation, clothing and textiles, home management, child care, and teacher training. Classes were held in several South Campus buildings until 1932, when Dawson Hall opened. It provided classrooms, labs, and studios for home economics courses and vocational training. That same year, the Division of Home Economics and a home economics department in the State Normal School were merged to form the School of Home Economics. The name was changed to College of Home Economics in 1979 and to College of Family and Consumer Sciences in 1990.

Dawson Hall is named for Dr. William Terrell Dawson, a Georgia native and grandson of William Terrell, the namesake of Terrell Hall on North Campus. Like his grandfather, Dawson, a physician, had a strong interest in farming and agricultural education; he willed an estate valued at about $150,000 to establish a trust in the College of Agriculture. The college used about $75,000 to build Dawson Hall. In addition to classrooms and laboratories, the building originally included a large cafeteria–banquet room and studios for design, weaving, pottery, metalwork, and other crafts. An annex added in 1971 is named for Mary Speirs, dean of the School of Home Economics from 1954 to 1971. The original building did not have the imposing Doric columns seen today, which were added in 1982 to provide a formal entrance. The college maintains a large collection of historic clothing, some of which is displayed in the building.

Soule Hall

BUILT: 1920 | NAMED FOR: Andrew M. Soule, dean of the College of Agriculture, president of the College of Agriculture and Mechanic Arts, 1907–32. | CURRENT USE: Residence hall for women | BUILDING 1220

Ground was broken for Soule Hall in 1918, the year women were officially admitted to UGA, and when it opened two years later as the first residence hall for females, it was named the Women's Building (though male students derisively called it the "Co-ed Barn"). The building was constructed partly with $100,000 that the state legislature allotted to create a College of Agriculture as part of the State College of Agriculture and Mechanic Arts headed by Andrew Soule, for whom the building was named in 1923. A&M College trustees supplemented the funding, and additional money was raised by selling naming rights for rooms in the building. The original building had a gymnasium, a swimming pool, classrooms, laboratories, parlors, a kitchen, and bedrooms for twenty female residents. The building served as a barracks for cadets in the navy preflight training school during World War II and after the war again housed female students. In 1972, despite protests from students and preservationists, it was leased to the State Department of Offender Rehabilitation as office and classroom space, but was returned four years later to being a women's dormitory. Closed in 1987 because of concerns about structural safety, the building underwent a major renovation that modernized the interior into a series of residential suites. Today Soule is the only all-female residence hall on South Campus and the oldest residence hall still used for its original purpose.

Andrew Soule was a vigorous champion of agricultural education, creating departments for agricultural chemistry, agronomy, forestry, horticulture, poultry, and veterinary science. An advocate of using the university's expertise to help citizens, he toured the state aboard a special train outfitted to demonstrate the newest developments in farming and agricultural technology. Soule's outreach initiatives laid the groundwork for the agricultural college's Cooperative Extension Service and, eventually, the university's massive public service program.

Early Female Students

Though they were college coeds, the first female students were bound by the social constraints of the time. Jennie Belle Myers, the housemother in Soule Hall, and Mary Lyndon, the first dean of women, enforced rules that forbade women to smoke in public or drink alcoholic beverages, required them to wear dresses or skirts and stockings on campus (except for bloomers for PE), and imposed strict curfew hours. Though heavily outnumbered by male students (many of whom opposed their admission), women gradually were accepted into campus life, working on the yearbook and newspaper staffs, participating in theatrical productions, and forming their own clubs, including a Student Government Association for Women. Women's intercollegiate athletic competition was still years away, but the female students competed among themselves on intramural teams in many sports, and those who excelled received a G monogram. Women were also excluded from army ROTC but formed a rifle team and received army instruction.

The opening of a chapter of the Phi Mu sorority in 1921, followed by Chi Omega in 1922, paved the way for the host of sororities that have become the center of much social life for women. Women outnumbered male students during World War II, though the disparity was less noticeable due to the presence of thousands of navy preflight cadets. The curfews, dress codes, and other conduct rules for women remained in force until the late 1960s, when the women's movement and student demonstrations led the university to drop its unofficial in loco parentis policy.

An Alpha Gamma Delta rush party, 1942

Sloth Skeleton

The foyer connecting the Science Library to the Boyd Graduate Studies Building is dominated by a skeleton of a giant North American ground sloth. Measuring about thirteen feet in length and weighing 2,500–3,000 pounds, the skeleton was reconstructed from bones unearthed in 1970 during construction of Interstate Highway 95 near Brunswick, Georgia. Many of the 350 bones were broken (or duplicates from other specimens), so nearly half the 208 bones in the skeleton are made of fiberglass or plaster of paris. Still, it is one of the most authentic re-creations of this late Ice Age relic and is the first skeleton of a prehistoric animal to be assembled in Georgia. When it was dedicated in 1973, it was only the fourth North American ground sloth known to have been mounted anywhere.

Science Library

BUILT: 1968 | BUILDING 1621

Opened as a strategic part of the Science Center complex, the Science Library supports research and teaching in a broad range of scientific fields, including agriculture, biological and life sciences, human and veterinary medicine, physical sciences, computer science, and technology. The library's holdings include more than 750,000 volumes, more than 3,000 print journals, and 19,000 full-text electronic journals.

Boyd Graduate Studies Building

BUILT: 1968 | NAMED FOR: George H. Boyd, dean of the Graduate School, 1943-59 | CURRENT USE: Office of the Vice President for Research, Department of Mathematics, Department of Computer Science, Institute for Artificial Intelligence, College of Engineering offices | BUILDING 1023

Although it didn't have a formal graduate school, UGA began offering post-graduate education after the Civil War. In 1870, three master of arts degrees were awarded (including one to the future UGA chancellor Walter Hill), and two decades later the master of science degree was offered. The Graduate School was established in 1910 with Willis Bocock, a classics professor, as the first dean and an initial offering of twelve graduate courses. The school grew steadily, and by the time the first PhD degree was presented in 1940, it was evolving into a comprehensive graduate program with a strong emphasis on research. Today more than sixty-five thousand graduate degrees have been awarded, and the school, with an enrollment of some seven thousand, ranks among the best graduate programs at U.S. public universities. The school's offices were on North Campus until this building opened. Erected over what was once a large natural amphitheater, the eight-story building is the tallest structure on the UGA campus. It once was the home of the computer center and housed a giant computer that was one of the most powerful in the country.

In 1972, the building was named for George H. Boyd, a native of Fairburn, Georgia, who came to UGA in 1926 to head the Zoology Department. A respected scientist, he stressed the importance of research for improving society and enhancing public welfare, and is credited with leading the Graduate School into the modern era. In 2007, Graduate School offices moved to a building in downtown Athens, but this building retains "Graduate Studies" in its name.

Marine Sciences / Dance Building

BUILT: 1928; expanded in 1969 | CURRENT USE: Department of Dance, Department of Marine Sciences, Marine Extension Program, Sea Grant Program | BUILDING 1030

A mix of architectural styles and academic disciplines, this building was erected for the women's health and physical education program, which began as part of the College of Agriculture in 1924. With its twenty-two-foot-high terra cotta Ionic columns and a traditional entablature consisting of cornice, frieze, and architrave, this imposing neoclassical revival building was the first on South Campus designed in a style that was common to the PWA buildings constructed a decade later. The original building had a basement swimming pool (which remains) and a large gymnasium, which also served as an auditorium with a capacity of twenty-five hundred. The gymnasium later became the first home of the women's gymnastics team. In 1969, a modern addition was joined to the building's western side by a brick-and-glass corridor. The addition more than doubled the building's size and provided more space for women's physical education, which included a growing dance program. When women's PE moved to the new Ramsey Center in 1995, dance became a separate department and took over the entire original building. The gymnasium was turned into a dance theater, and other spaces became dance studios. The western addition was converted into classrooms, laboratories, and research space for marine studies, outreach, and the Sea Grant Program. This is the only academic building in which a performing arts department and a science department share space.

Snelling Hall

BUILT: 1940 | NAMED FOR: Charles M. Snelling, UGA chancellor, 1926–32 | CURRENT USE: Student dining hall | BUILDING 1643

Another PWA building, Snelling Hall was constructed as a dining facility and has always been used for that purpose. The Georgian Revival building features an entranceway with tall Doric columns topped by a broken pediment crowned by a pineapple, a traditional sign of hospitality. By the 1970s, the building had outgrown its initial capacity of seven hundred, and wings were added on the north and west. An $800,000 renovation in 2001–2 added food

lines and made other improvements that expanded capacity to three thousand. The facility is open around-the-clock on weekdays during the fall and spring semesters.

Charles Snelling was the last man to hold the title of chancellor of the University of Georgia, but he retained the title when he was appointed the first chancellor of the University System of Georgia in 1932. He came to UGA from the Virginia Military Institute to teach mathematics and command the military cadet corps, and served as dean before becoming chancellor. His tenure at UGA's helm was marked by important changes in entrance and degree requirements, a nearly one-third increase in enrollment, and several major construction projects, including Sanford Stadium.

College of Family and Consumer Sciences McPhaul Center

BUILT: 1939 | NAMED FOR: Margaret McPhaul, an early leader in child development at UGA | CURRENT USE: Research units of the College of Family and Consumer Sciences and the McPhaul Child Development Laboratory | BUILDINGS 1246, 1247, 1248, 1249, 1652

This cluster of five buildings, constructed for $120,000, including funds from PWA grants, began as "home management laboratories" for the School of Home Economics. Four of the buildings were designed as typical family homes, with a fully furnished living room, dining room, bedrooms, bathrooms, and laundry facilities. Seniors in the home economics school lived in the houses for an academic quarter, learning such household skills as budgeting, meal planning and preparation, decorating, and maintenance. A fifth building opened in 1940 as the Nursery School, a preschool for young children that was also a teaching and training laboratory for home economics students studying child development. The school was started in 1928 and operated in another building before moving to this facility, which had such innovations as observation booths, testing rooms with two-way windows, and pediatric and psychiatric services. The building still houses a high-demand preschool program.

In 1971, the building was enlarged and two years later was named the McPhaul Child Development Laboratory in honor of Margaret E. McPhaul, the director of the school from 1937 to 1964. It also houses a program named ASPIRE, which provides counseling for individuals, couples, and families on such topics as nutrition, financial management, mental health, interpersonal relationships, and legal problems. The home management training program in the four smaller houses ended in 1989, and the buildings were converted to offices for faculty members and research programs that focus on families, consumer habits, housing, and demographics.

The Gardens at Athens

BUILT: 1982 | CURRENT USE: Teaching and research on plants | BUILDING 1340 (Horticultural Greenhouse)

The acclaimed UGA plant scientists Allan Armitage and Michael Dirr and their students started this garden, originally called the UGA Horticulture Trial Garden, to introduce new plants and study their growth. Each spring scores of annual and perennial species, including many specialty varieties, are planted. Students tend the beds, and every two weeks each cultivar is evaluated for such characteristics as number of flowers, leaf color, resistance to insects and disease, tolerance of heat and humidity, and overall appearance. Data are used to chart the overall performance of plants from spring till fall, and each plant receives a performance rating. At the end of each growing season, garden personnel select the dozen best cultivars to receive the Classic City Garden Award. Information from the tests is available to breeders, growers, retailers, landscapers, and consumers. Brilliant with summer color, the gardens attract insects and birds and provide a soothing respite from busy campus life.

Robert Wilson Pharmacy Building

BUILT: 1964 | NAMED FOR: Robert C. Wilson, dean of School of Pharmacy, 1917–49 | CURRENT USE: College of Pharmacy | BUILDING 1041

Shortly after the School of Pharmacy was established in 1903, its home in Science Hall on North Campus burned to the ground. Terrell Hall, built over the ruins, housed the school from 1905 until 1939, when it moved to New College. In 1964, the school became the last science unit to leave North Campus, moving to this modernist building to join the other science units on South Campus. The building, with a footprint the size of a football field, has a design, novel at the time, featuring a glass-walled corridor around the outside, with offices and laboratories occupying interior space.

The building was named in 1978 for Robert Wilson on the occasion of his one-hundredth birthday. Wilson, who attended the dedication, joined the school in 1907 as an instructor. He became dean in 1917 when the school's first dean died and went on to serve thirty-three years. Dubbed the "Father of Pharmacy in Georgia" for his pioneering efforts to improve pharmacy education and practice, Wilson created one of the first four-year bachelor of science degree programs in pharmacy and was largely responsible for establishing educational requirements for pharmacy licensure. He helped write a Georgia law that became the model for national legislation prohibiting the sale of narcotics without a prescription, and he was a leader in state and national pharmacy organizations. He died in Athens in 1981 at the age of 102. In the building's main lobby is a re-creation of Wilson's office, complete with a 1913 calendar; several mortars and pestles and other old pharmacy equipment and medicines; an antique radio and books; and the desk and chair Wilson bought himself because the school didn't have money to furnish his office.

Pharmacy South

BUILT: 2010 | CURRENT USE: College of Pharmacy classrooms and laboratories | BUILDING 1038

Having long outgrown its space in the Wilson Building, the College of Pharmacy welcomed the opening of this $44 million, 93,288-square-foot structure. Replete with advanced technological and environmental features, it was the first UGA building to be registered for LEED certification, the national benchmark for design, construction, and operation of high-performance green buildings. The building's emergency generator is biodiesel powered, and energy use is significantly reduced by integrating the chemical fume hoods in labs with the central heating and air-conditioning system. A fifteen-thousand-gallon underwater cistern captures rain and condensate water for reuse in irrigating the nearby landscape. A portion of

the roof is used as a "green roof" covered with grass, flowers, and other small plants. High ceilings, tall windows, and uncluttered gathering spaces create an airy, inviting atmosphere that encourages interaction among faculty and students. Classrooms and labs have video-recording and distance-learning capabilities and wireless Internet computer stations. A Community Pharmacy Care Center and a Hospital Pharmacy Care Center simulate real-life facilities in order to give students hands-on training in treating patients.

D. W. Brooks Mall

BUILT: 2001–6 | NAMED FOR: D. W. Brooks, a Georgia agribusiness pioneer

This placid, parklike mall was created as part of an environmentally focused master plan that envisioned an area of green space on South Campus similar to the North Campus quadrangles. For decades, South Campus was bisected by a narrow, congested street named D. W. Brooks Drive, which ran from Cedar Street to Carlton Street. In 2001, workers began tearing out the street and adjacent sidewalks and parking lots and replacing the asphalt and concrete with this expanse of lush lawns and native trees, shrubs, and flowers. At the mall's north end is a large ellipse of open green space and a formal walled garden that hark back to the area's agricultural roots. The cornstalk pattern on the fence at the mall's south end reflects UGA's status as the nation's fourth-largest center for corn research. In addition to its beautification benefits, the mall helps reduce the heat-island effect caused by concrete and asphalt, increases storm drainage capacity, and improves irrigation.

The mall's namesake, D. W. Brooks, formed a farm cooperative in 1933 that became Gold Kist, Inc., one of the nation's largest poultry-processing operations. He later started Cotton States Mutual Insurance Companies to provide farmers with fire and storm insurance. Brooks earned a bachelor's degree in science from UGA in 1922 and a master's degree the next year; he taught for several years before going into business. An adviser to seven U.S. presidents, he was a trustee of the UGA Foundation, the first inductee into the UGA Agriculture Hall of Fame, and Georgia's Man of the Year in Agriculture in 1955.

Lumpkin House

BUILT: 1844 | NAMED FOR: Wilson Lumpkin, Georgia governor (1831–35), U.S. senator (1838–41) | CURRENT USE: College of Agricultural and Environmental Sciences | BUILDING 1012

Contrasting starkly with nearby modern science buildings, this quaint structure—also known as "Rock House"—is the oldest building on South Campus and probably still stands only because of an odd clause in a deed. After serving as a congressman, two-term governor, and U.S. senator, Wilson Lumpkin retired to Athens and built this home on land he purchased from the university atop a rise called Cedar Hill. Lumpkin personally designed the house—supposedly to resemble a millhouse that was one of the first buildings in Athens—and brought in a stonecutter from Ireland, a woodworker from New Jersey, and a painter from England. Lumpkin said of the structure, "I endeavored to put a piece of my character into its stone walls." Adhering to a superstition that forecasts an early death for anyone who completely finishes a new house, Lumpkin left one window unfinished—and perhaps fulfilled the myth by living to the age of eighty-seven.

Lumpkin's youngest daughter, Martha Lumpkin Compton, inherited the house and sold it to UGA in 1907, along with twenty-two acres of land that became the site of adjacent Conner Hall. But the sale had an unusual stipulation: if the university ever moved or destroyed the house, both the land the house sat on and the surrounding acreage would revert to her heirs. The university has honored the provision. The house has been used for classrooms, student housing, a branch library, a computer center, and the headquarters of the Institute of Ecology. In 1970, it was listed on the National Register of Historic Places.

Conner Hall

BUILT: 1908 | NAMED FOR: James J. Conner, a state legislator who supported agricultural education | CURRENT USE: College of Agricultural and Environmental Sciences | BUILDING 1011

Conner Hall, originally known as Agricultural Hall, is the second-oldest building on South Campus (following Lumpkin House) and the first built for academic purposes. Sited on one of the highest elevations in Athens, it was erected in the Renaissance Revival style to house the university's new College of Agriculture, created in 1906 as part of the Georgia State College of Agriculture and Mechanic Arts. Although part of the university, the agriculture college operated as an independent school, and the building was purposely sited apart from North Campus as a sign of that separation. The original building—the first on campus with central heating—had sixty rooms, which were used as classrooms, laboratories, and offices for a dozen departments, including agronomy, horticulture, cotton, dairy, veterinary medicine, and entomology.

Over the years the building has also housed a library, auditorium, cafeteria, creamery, and the studio for a daily farm program broadcast on the radio in the 1920s and 1930s. By the mid-1970s, the building's sturdy brick masonry and limestone walls were still strong, but the interior, which had undergone many changes, was outdated and out of compliance with fire codes and accessibility requirements. In a $2.6 million renovation begun in 1975, the inside was gutted and rebuilt with modern touches, including elevators and a more efficient heating and cooling system. The historic exterior was little changed except for the addition of tinted windows. A display in the lobby traces the history of the Cooperative Extension Service and the College of Agricultural and Environmental Sciences from the 1890s.

James Conner, a state legislator, wrote the bill that created the College of Agriculture and helped secure a $100,000 appropriation from the General Assembly to construct the building. He was head of the college's board of trustees and later served as state commissioner of agriculture. Conner Hall remains the nerve center of UGA's vast program of agricultural education, research, and outreach.

Barrow Hall

BUILT: 1911 | NAMED FOR: David C. Barrow, UGA chancellor, 1906–25 |
CURRENT USE: Center for Ultrastructural Research, Institute for Behavioral Research,
Institute for Health Management and Mass Destruction Defense, units of the
College of Family and Consumer Sciences | BUILDING 1021

Constructed for the College of Agriculture, Barrow Hall is the third-oldest building on South Campus. The first wing, completed in 1911 and called the Farm Mechanics Building, housed the college's agricultural engineering and forestry programs. A second wing, known as the Agricultural Engineering Building, was added in 1916. The building has been twice enlarged, and its interior has been reconfigured for many purposes, including offices, classrooms, laboratories, and woodworking and blacksmithing shops. A wing behind the building houses the Center for Ultrastructural Research, and two adjacent small buildings are home to a food-processing lab and a School of Ecology annex.

Barrow Hall was constructed during the tenure of Chancellor David Barrow and named for him in 1923. A beloved leader, "Uncle Dave," as he was affectionately known, was descended from three generations of university trustees. An 1874 graduate and a faculty member for forty-six years, he was head of the Engineering and Mathematics Departments and dean of the College of Arts and Sciences before being elected chancellor in 1906. Barrow and his predecessor, Walter B. Hill, helped transform the university from a liberal arts college into a true university.

Hardman Hall

BUILT: 1922 | NAMED FOR: Lamartine G. Hardman, Georgia governor, 1927–31 | CURRENT USE: Air force ROTC | BUILDING 1031

Construction of this building began in 1918 and was completed four years later. Built to house the College of Agriculture's Animal Husbandry Department, the building originally contained a livestock arena where cattle shows were held. Following World War I, it was headquarters for a program the university sponsored to help educate war veterans. In 1946, the agriculture college housed its revived veterinary medicine program, which had been shut down thirteen years earlier, in this building, and later it was used by the women's physical education department. The air force ROTC program has been here since 1971.

Lamartine Hardman, born in 1856 near Commerce, Georgia, was a prominent physician, businessman, and farmer. A state legislator from 1902 to 1907, he was Georgia's fuel administrator during World War I and in 1926 became the state's oldest elected governor at age seventy-one. One of his accomplishments was to initiate a study of government efficiency that led to a major reorganization of state government under his successor, Richard Russell. Hardman was chair of the University Trustees Executive Committee for twenty-five years and was also a trustee of Mercer University.

Statistics / EITS / Museum of Natural History

BUILT: around 1958 | CURRENT USE: Department of Statistics, Enterprise Information
Technology Services, Georgia Museum of Natural History | BUILDING 1130

Originally part of the university's Physical Plant division, which occupied this
area for many years, this building has been repeatedly added to and renovated.
A portion of the building once served as a garage for buses and trucks. It has
been used primarily for offices since the 1970s, and since 1990 has housed
some collections of the Georgia Museum of Natural History.

The museum is headquartered in this building, but its fourteen collections
of archaeological, biological, geological, and paleontological materials are
scattered among different locations on and off campus and are largely unavail-
able for public view because of space limitations. The more than five million
objects in the collections constitute the most comprehensive inventory available of Georgia's cultural, biological, and geological heritage. The collections
are an invaluable storehouse of information for teaching and research at UGA
and for promoting environmental education, conservation, biodiversity, and
habitat protection. The collections include fungi, fish, insects, amphibians,
reptiles, birds, mammals, plants, rocks, minerals, fossils, pottery, and other
archaeological artifacts. Each collection is the largest of its kind in the state
(the archaeological collection alone has more than three million artifacts, and

the arthropod collection totals more than one million specimens), and some are among the largest in the South. With materials dating back thousands of years, some of the collections are historical records of locations and species that are extinct, rare, or endangered.

Many collections were started decades ago by faculty members and students and are maintained today by academic departments as resources for teaching and research. UGA created the Georgia Museum of Natural History in 1978 to provide administrative support for the collections and to coordinate their use. In 1999, the Georgia General Assembly designated the museum the state's official museum of natural history. The museum headquarters includes a small public exhibition space that is open weekdays from nine to five. Information about tours, programs, and museum activities is available on the museum website, http://museum.nhm.uga.edu.

Ecology Building

BUILT: 1974 | CURRENT USE: Eugene Odum School of Ecology | BUILDING 1033

Often called the "father of modern ecology," Eugene Odum was associated with UGA for more than half a century. He earned international recognition for groundbreaking research on ecosystems and was instrumental in thrusting the university to the forefront in research and teaching on ecological and environmental matters. In 1960, he founded the Institute of Ecology, which in 2007 became the Odum School of Ecology, the world's first stand-alone school devoted to ecological teaching and research. Adhering to Odum's holistic philosophy for understanding ecosystems, the school—consistently ranked among the nation's top ten—emphasizes an interdisciplinary approach to research in such areas as infectious diseases, watershed ecology, evolutionary ecology, and sustainability. This building, twice enlarged since its construction, has a bronze bust of Odum in the lobby and includes laboratories, offices, a 130-seat auditorium–classroom, and a central landscaped courtyard.

Forestry and Natural Resources Building

BUILT: 1938 | CURRENT USE: Warnell School of Forestry and Natural Resources | BUILDINGS 1040, 1140, 1044, 1046

Created in 1906 with a gift from the philanthropist George Foster Peabody, the Warnell School of Forestry and Natural Resources is the oldest existing forestry school in the South. It began as a department in the State College of Agriculture and Mechanic Arts and remained in the College of Agriculture until 1935, when the University System of Georgia authorized the creation of a School of Forestry. This PWA-funded structure, constructed at a cost of $120,000, was dubbed the "classic" forestry building for its stately appearance featuring a triangular pediment and four towering Doric columns. A forestry motif is reflected in offices, halls, and classrooms, which are paneled in rich dark wood from native cypress, pine, and white oak trees. Plaques in the building honor forestry students killed in World War II and subsequent conflicts.

The original building has expanded into a four-building complex with state-of-the-art facilities and equipment for teaching and research. The school's name was changed in 1968 to the School of Forest Resources and in 2006 to the School of Forestry and Natural Resources to better reflect its broadened mission. In 1991, the school was named for Daniel B. Warnell, a Georgia native involved in banking, farming, and timber management. As a state legislator

The Forestry School "Student Revolt"

In its early years, having only a few students and faculty, the forestry program struggled to stay afloat. It was shuffled from building to building with no permanent home. In 1937, it was lodged in a dilapidated structure that had been abandoned by the defunct veterinary medicine program. When the forestry dean resigned in frustration over poor support for the program, forestry students angrily threatened to strike. President Harmon Caldwell's promise to put a new forestry building on an emergency list for the board of regents did not deter a group of students from converging on the governor's office in Atlanta to protest the school's poor facilities and treatment. The governor sent them to the board of regents, who, outraged by the students' audacity, rejected their pleas. Undaunted, the students published a pamphlet that branded their building a "dog house" and suggested that the school's accreditation might be revoked because of its poor facilities and low faculty salaries. The students' protest and pamphlet drew statewide attention, including coverage in the Atlanta newspapers, and led state and university officials to authorize a new building for the forestry school.

in the 1930s, Warnell supported rural development, public education, and the conservation of natural resources. The small garden adjacent to the building, named the Mary Kars Warnell Memory Garden in honor of Daniel Warnell's wife, features tall river birch trees, native shrubs and wildflowers, and a pool with native water plants.

Environmental Health Science Building

BUILT: 1939 | CURRENT USE: Department of Environmental Health Science, Creamery | BUILDING 1050

This building was constructed with PWA funds to house the Dairy Science Department, a unit of the College of Agriculture. The seventy-five-hundred-square-foot structure, designed in the neoclassical revival style with Roman Doric columns, originally had exterior stairs on both ends and contained laboratories, lecture halls, classrooms, and offices. In the mid-1950s, dairy science merged with animal husbandry, another unit of the agricultural college, to form the Division of Animal Science. When this unit moved to the new Rhodes Center for Animal and Dairy Science in 1998, the building became the home of the Department of Environmental Health Science, a unit of the College of Public Health. More than half the space is devoted to laboratories for research in aquatic and environmental toxicology, environmental microbiology and chemistry, and air quality. The remainder of the building contains classrooms and offices.

Tucked into the south side of the building is the Creamery, a small eatery that has been part of UGA for more than a century. Started in 1908 to process milk from the university dairy farm, it was located in Conner Hall until moving to this building in 1941. For many years the Creamery sold fresh milk, cream, cheese, butter, and ice cream produced from cows at the university dairy farm; in fact, it was a main source of dairy products in Athens. Today it is part of University Food Services and sells sandwiches, soups, pastries, snacks, drinks, and ice cream in a variety of flavors. The Creamery is open Monday–Friday, 8:00 a.m.–5:00 p.m.

Fred C. Davison Life Sciences Complex

BUILT: 1991 | NAMED FOR: Fred C. Davison, UGA president, 1967–86 | CURRENT USE:
Department of Genetics, Department of Biochemistry and Molecular Biology | BUILDING 1057

Three deteriorating buildings (Fain, Dudley, and Griggs Halls), erected in the
early 1940s to house navy preflight school cadets, were razed to make way for
this 257,000-square-foot structure, the largest construction project in the history of the University System of Georgia when it opened in 1991. Touted for its
modern design, the $32 million building features a trio of connected, octag-
onally shaped towers containing eighty laboratories, as well as classrooms,
offices, and support space. The Genetics and Biochemistry Departments are
pillars of UGA's internationally respected leadership in life sciences research,
an area that includes biomedicine, genetic engineering, biofuels, molecular
modeling, genomics, and bioinformatics.

In 2004, the building was named for Fred Davison, the university's eighteenth president, who made scientific research a top priority by emphasizing
the then-emerging field of biotechnology. Davison recruited leading scientists
to the faculty and oversaw a sixfold increase in the research budget. His initiatives are credited with catapulting UGA into the top ranks of U.S. research
universities.

As an undergraduate student at the University of Georgia, I was introduced to social work during a summer session—and made an A+! The MSW program chartered my professional career in social work. I then returned as a professor of social work and coordinator of the certificate program in marriage and family therapy. While there, I had an office on the third floor of Tucker Hall. The windows were open one night when I was working late during a summer session, and all of a sudden I sneezed hard. Far down below on the street, I heard someone yell back, "Bless you!" I guess that said something about the strength of my sneezes, and also about the strength of camaraderie on campus! That camaraderie carried over to faculty relationships and also to faculty-staff-student relationships. It made my going on twenty-five years on the faculty a most pleasant and memorable experience. As a retired faculty member of the University of Georgia School of Social Work, I am proud to be a graduate and professor emerita.

Allie Callaway Kilpatrick-Hill, MSW, 1966

Tucker Hall

BUILT: 1961 | NAMED FOR: Henry H. Tucker, UGA chancellor, 1874–78 | CURRENT USE: School of Social Work | BUILDING 1250

Tucker Hall is one of nine residence halls built in the early 1960s to accommodate the rapidly growing student body. Eight of the buildings were located on the campus's western edge, but Tucker was placed on South Campus for the convenience of male students studying agriculture. It served that purpose until 1974, when it was converted into office and classroom space for the School of Social Work. Henry Tucker, born in Warren County, was the first native Georgian to lead the university. A lawyer and Baptist minister, he had been president of Mercer University, and one of his major challenges as chancellor was to fend off efforts by the state's denominational colleges to siphon resources from UGA. Opinionated and outspoken, he feuded with university trustees over the curriculum and student discipline; as a result, he was eased out after only four years. The School of Social Work, started in 1964, was the last school created at UGA until 2001. The master of social work program ranks in the top 25 percent of MSW programs nationwide. The school is home of the Foot Soldier Project for Civil Rights Studies and Research.

Miller Plant Sciences Building / Alan Jaworski Plant Science Amphitheater

BUILT: 1972 | NAMED FOR: Julian H. Miller, a pioneering professor of plant pathology | CURRENT USE: Departments of Plant Biology, Horticulture, Crop and Soil Science, and Plant Pathology | BUILDING 1061

Agriculture and related fields are a multibillion-dollar industry for Georgia, and UGA scientists are in the forefront of developing new knowledge to strengthen this economic sector. Scientists in this building conduct advanced research that covers the full spectrum of plant life, from molecules to ecosystems. Studies are directed toward understanding the scientific principles and mechanisms that control plant growth, and toward applying techniques and measures to improve plant health and yield. Research focuses on ways to increase production of such important Georgia crops as peaches, pecans, peanuts, and onions; techniques to prevent and manage plant diseases and pests; ways to enhance and conserve soil; and advances in landscape plant selection, propagation, and production. On the second floor is the UGA Herbarium, a collection of more than 260,000 dried, pressed, and mounted plant specimens representing virtually every plant species in Georgia. A part of UGA's Museum of Natural History, the herbarium was started in the 1920s and includes specimens dating from the 1800s. It is the largest herbarium in Georgia and one of the largest in the Southeast. It includes the Julian H. Miller Mycological Collection, which comprises more than thirty thousand specimens of fungi.

Julian Miller, a faculty member from 1919 to 1958, became the first chair of the Plant Pathology Department in 1932. A world authority in the field of mycology, he discovered information that led to new scientific classifications of certain kinds of fungi.

On the north side of the building is the Alan Jaworski Plant Science Amphitheater, which is frequented for reading, studying, outdoor classes, and meetings. Jaworski, who died in 2000, was a popular professor and department head in the Plant Biology Department; during a twenty-eight-year tenure, he taught thousands of students in introductory biology courses.

Plant Genetics at UGA

UGA geneticists designed a gene that, when inserted into plants, can remove heavy metal pollutants such as mercury and lead from soil and render them harmless.

Aderhold Hall

BUILT: 1971 | NAMED FOR: Omer Clyde (O. C.) Aderhold, UGA president, 1950–67 | CURRENT USE: College of Education | BUILDING 1060

Seven-story Aderhold Hall, encompassing 201,062 square feet, was one of the largest buildings on campus when it opened in 1971 as home of the College of Education, which had been in cramped space on North Campus. The building had 225 offices, 33 classrooms, 11 conference rooms, and 18 laboratories. A library contains curriculum materials for grades K–12 and a large collection of juvenile literature. Spaces were designed to enable the college for the first

time to provide training for students in specialized areas of education. But the building was not without flaws. The escalator—the first on campus—frequently malfunctioned, and eventually was disabled and turned into stairs. Many interior offices and rooms have no windows, and the building was designed so that in case of fire, hallway doors would close to prevent drafts. Lights were hooked into the same system, so when the first fire drill was held, doors automatically shut and lights went out, leaving the people in interior offices trapped in darkness. An auxiliary lighting system was soon installed. Despite its size, the building still was not large enough for all the college's departments, and several were dispersed among other buildings. With almost five thousand students and about two hundred faculty members, the college today is UGA's second largest and one of the largest education colleges in the country. Several highly ranked departments and a faculty of international stature make the college a leader in instruction, research, and outreach.

O. C. Aderhold was dean of the college from 1946 until 1950, when he became the university's seventeenth president, a post he held until 1967. Under Aderhold, UGA was racially integrated and began to be transformed from a small state university into one of regional significance as enrollment more than doubled, graduate and professional programs were strengthened, and more than a dozen buildings were constructed.

Paul Coverdell Center for Biomedical and Health Sciences

BUILT: 2006 | NAMED FOR: Paul Coverdell, U.S. senator, 1992–2000 | CURRENT USE: Biomedical and Health Sciences Institute, other life sciences research programs | BUILDING IIII

The Coverdell Center is the signature component of UGA's burgeoning initiative for research, education, and development related to new technology in biomedicine, health, and life sciences. In its 172,180 square feet are laboratories and other facilities for some 275 scientists, staff members, and graduate students working in such areas as infectious diseases, developmental biology, regenerative medicine, and public health. The building's open "flex labs" and meeting spaces are designed to encourage scientists from different disciplines to interact and collaborate on research. Constructed from indigenous granite and some recycled materials, the building was among the first on campus to incorporate environmentally friendly features such as sensors that cut off lights in empty rooms and a forty-thousand-gallon-cistern that captures

Alfred Blalock

Alfred Blalock, who graduated in 1918, was a pioneering surgeon who helped develop a shunt technique for heart bypass that opened the way for the modern field of heart surgery. He also helped develop a surgical technique to treat the heart condition known as blue baby syndrome.

storm water runoff and air-conditioning condensate for irrigation and toilet flushing. The building's traditional architectural style, featuring an entrance encircled by tall columns, along with the scenic garden in the rear, reflects the historic character of North Campus.

The U.S. Congress and the Georgia General Assembly each appropriated $10 million for the building in honor of Paul Coverdell, who was a Georgia state senator before serving as director of the Peace Corps and being elected to the U.S. Senate. UGA raised an additional $20 million from private sources. Former president George H. W. Bush spoke at the building's grand opening in 2006.

Veterinary Medicine Building

BUILT: 1949 | CURRENT USE: College of Veterinary Medicine | BUILDING 1070

The university's veterinary program began in 1918 as part of the College of Agriculture, but was discontinued in 1933 when the University System of Georgia was formed. A growing demand for veterinary skills in Georgia and the Southeast after World War II led to the program's revival in 1946 with creation of the School (now College) of Veterinary Medicine. The Veterinary Medicine Building was constructed on the north edge of Camp Wilkins as

the first structure in a complex that grew to include an annex (added in 1973), the Teaching Hospital (built in 1979), a diagnostic lab (opened in 2001), and the Animal Health Research Center (started in 2006). In 2012, work began on a $100 million state-of-the-art facility for the Teaching Hospital located on College Station Road off campus. The college—one of only twenty-eight in the country and eight in the Southeast—has a contractual arrangement to serve primarily students from Georgia, South Carolina, West Virginia, and Delaware.

An international leader in veterinary education, research, and service, the college is equipped with the most advanced technology for training students in diagnostic, treatment, and health management skills for large and small animals. Faculty members conduct research on infectious diseases, wildlife diseases, parasitic diseases, vaccines, and equine colic. The Animal Health Research Center, the only agricultural lab certified for biosafety level 3 containment on a U.S. university campus, is the site of groundbreaking studies on dangerous animal-borne diseases that can also infect humans. The Poultry Diagnostic and Research Center is a world leader in developing products to prevent and treat poultry diseases. The Southeastern Cooperative Wildlife Disease Study provides fifteen states with diagnostic services for mammals, birds, reptiles, and amphibians.

Faculty members in the Teaching Hospital have expertise in all areas of animal medicine, including surgery, radiology, dermatology, urology, and reproduction. Students, interns, and residents work alongside hospital faculty members to treat nearly nineteen thousand dogs, horses, cats, birds, and other animals annually, using diagnostic techniques and treatments possible only in a hospital setting. The hospital serves farmers and assists private practitioners throughout the state and provides care and treatment for exotic animals at nearby zoos.

Driftmier Engineering Center

BUILT: 1966 | NAMED FOR: Rudolph H. Driftmier, a campus engineer and the head of the Agricultural Engineering Division in the College of Agriculture | CURRENT USE: College of Engineering | BUILDING 1090

Engineering has been taught at UGA since the 1830s. An engineering school begun after the Civil War awarded its first engineering degrees in 1868. The school became part of the College of Agriculture when it was created in 1906, but when the University System of Georgia was formed in 1932, all UGA

engineering programs except agricultural engineering were transferred to Georgia Tech. Agricultural engineering, later called biological and agricultural engineering, remained a mainstay in the agricultural college over the years; other fields of engineering were incorporated into various nonagricultural departments and disciplines.

Eventually, twenty-five departments in eight colleges offered some kind of engineering instruction, and in 2001 a Faculty of Engineering was formed to foster an interdisciplinary approach to engineering teaching, research, and outreach. The faculty received approval from the board of regents in 2007 to become an institute with the authority to offer degree programs in biochemical engineering, computer systems engineering, and environmental engineering. Three years later, the regents approved degree programs in civil engineering, electrical and electronics engineering, and mechanical engineering. In 2012, when 540 undergraduates and 55 graduate students were enrolled in engineering classes, the regents approved merging the Faculty of Engineering and the Biological and Agricultural Engineering Department to create a College of Engineering offering undergraduate, master's, and doctoral degrees. Intense demand for engineering education in Georgia is expected to drive enrollment in the college to nearly 1,200 by 2015.

The 110,000-square-foot Driftmier Center, with classrooms, labs, and offices, was built to house biological and agricultural engineering, and now is headquarters for the engineering college. Some of the building's classrooms have video- or computer-based projection systems, and one has a dedicated computer network for interactive and collaborative instruction. A 7,000-square-foot annex houses offices and labs for engineering outreach.

The building was named in 1982 for Rudolph Driftmier, who was a College of Agriculture faculty member from 1930 to 1965 and led the Division of Agricultural Engineering for most of those years. A working engineer, Driftmier partnered with Roy Hitchcock, an architect, to design and over-see construction of more than fifteen buildings at UGA, including many of the federally funded PWA buildings constructed in the late 1930s. Driftmier was also the supervising engineer for the University System and, along with Hitchcock, helped create eighty buildings at sixteen schools in the System.

R. Chappelle Matthews Public Service Complex

Located along the southwest border of campus on Lumpkin Street are build-ings that house units of UGA's public service and outreach program. The university's designations as a land-grant institution and a Sea Grant insti-tution require UGA to use its resources and expertise to help solve problems and improve life for Georgians. Its public service program has become one of the largest and most far-reaching in the country. One of the earliest outreach efforts was the College on Wheels, organized in the early twentieth century. Andrew Soule, president of the College of Agriculture and Mechanic Arts, and college faculty members traveled around Georgia on a chartered train, reach-ing hundreds of thousands of citizens with lectures and demonstrations on the newest tools and techniques for "scientific agriculture." Chancellor Walter Hill strongly advocated extending the university's reach into the state, and the federal Smith-Lever Act of 1914 gave public service a major boost by creating an agricultural extension service. By 1920, UGA's extension service had 80 male county agents and 62 female home demonstration workers in the field, and the total stood at 286 a decade later.

In the 1920s and 1930s, university personnel began providing assistance to state and local governmental agencies through the Institute of Public Affairs, which became the Vinson Institute of Government, as well as offering corre-spondence courses. With the opening of the Georgia Center for Continuing Education in the mid-1950s, and the appointment of the first vice president for public service in 1965, public service solidified its place as a core university priority. Today more than five hundred faculty and staff members work in all 159 Georgia counties and more than five hundred cities, providing information, resources, and technical assistance to help communities in such areas as governmental services and operations, economic development, education, environmental issues, marine industries, health, and recreation. A study in 2012 estimated that UGA's public service program has an annual economic impact of $330 million on the state, including supporting 3,370 jobs.

Chappelle Matthews, an Athens native and 1933 UGA graduate, practiced law in Athens and served in the Georgia House of Representatives from 1949 to 1976. As longtime chair of the University System Committee, he earned the titles "Mr. Higher Education" and "Mr. University System" for his efforts on behalf of UGA and other colleges. He retired from the House as its longest-serving member. He received UGA's Outstanding Alumni Award and Distinguished Service Award. Matthews died in 1986, and in 2011 the university recognized his contributions by placing his bust in front of the Treanor House. The bronze statue was created by Jack Kehoe, a UGA art professor.

The Matthews Public Service Complex includes the Georgia Center for Continuing Education, the Hoke Smith Building / Hoke Smith Annex, the J. W. Fanning Building, and the Treanor House.

Georgia Center for Continuing Education Conference Center and Hotel

BUILT: 1957 | CURRENT USE: Continuing education programs for professional development and personal enrichment | BUILDING 1640

Some one hundred thousand people pass through the doors of this building each year, making it one of the busiest on campus. Most come to attend conferences, seminars, workshops, and other professional development programs, though the center is also heavily used for community events and university functions. UGA received a $2 million grant from the Kellogg Foundation in 1953 to create the center—at the time the largest gift the foundation had made to a state university. The state supplemented the grant with $1.9 million. Several expansions, including an addition funded in 1984 by $15 million from Kellogg and $7 million from the state, enlarged the center to 288,594 square feet, making it one of the largest university-based continuing education facilities in the country. In addition to hosting professional development programs, the center offers adult education opportunities through community short

Located in the Georgia Center for Continuing Education, WUGA, the university's public radio station, broadcasts music, news, and information around the clock to Athens and portions of Northeast Georgia. A member station of Georgia Public Broadcasting and an affiliate of National Public Radio, WUGA signed on the air on August 28, 1987, fulfilling a dream envisioned thirty years earlier. Original floor plans for the Georgia Center, which opened in 1957, included a radio station. Those plans were sidetracked by other priorities, but the rising popularity of public radio after NPR was started in 1971 pushed UGA officials to add the university to a growing list of universities and metropolitan areas with public radio stations. The station became a reality when a 1984 grant from the W. K. Kellogg Foundation to expand the Georgia Center included funding specifically for a public radio station. With an estimated weekly audience of about twenty-five thousand, WUGA is third among eighteen reporting stations in the Athens area in number of listeners. Classical music has always been a staple of the station's format, occupying about half of its daily airtime. The remainder is devoted to news and public affairs, jazz, folk music, and comedy and drama. WUGA staff members produce nearly half the station's programming, including shows focusing on local news, the Athens music scene, folk music, and alternative music. *African Perspectives*, a show about African culture and music hosted by Akinloye Ojo, a UGA professor, has been on the air more than fifteen years and is believed to be one of the longest-running public radio shows of its kind in the country. The station has won dozens of national and state awards for news coverage and local programming, and some of its locally produced shows are carried on the GPB radio network. WUGA occasionally brings favorite NPR shows such as *Mountain Stage* and *From the Top* to Athens, and recordings of concert performances by internationally known artists in the UGA Performing Arts Center are regularly aired on the NPR show *Performance Today*. The station has been a training ground for staff members who moved on to successful careers with NPR and other public radio networks and stations.

courses, teacher certification courses, and instruction through teleconferences and audioconferences. Conferees and campus visitors can stay in the center's two hundred comfortable hotel rooms (one of which is reserved for the university's bulldog mascot, Uga) and enjoy gourmet fare in the Savannah Room restaurant. The studios of WUGA, the university's National Public Radio affiliate, are in the building.

Hoke Smith Building / Hoke Smith Annex

NAMED FOR: Hoke Smith, Georgia governor (1907–9, 1911) and U.S. senator (1911–21) | BUILT: 1937, 1940 | CURRENT USE: Cooperative Extension Service, Office of Global Programs, Office of International Agriculture | BUILDING 1042

The Hoke Smith Building, called Hoke Smith Hall when it opened in 1937, was one of the first PWA-financed buildings at UGA. It initially housed the Agricultural Extension Service, Soil Conservation Service, Farm Security Administration, and other agriculture-related agencies. The building's neoclassical revival architecture features an imposing entrance portico with four Corinthian columns of a type known as "temple of the winds." A mosaic map of Georgia is embedded in the porch tile. As the extension service grew, it displaced other occupants, and today most of the building houses offices of the Cooperative Extension Service, a unit of the College of Agricultural and Environmental Sciences. The Hoke Smith Annex, built in 1940 with substantial financial support from the city of Athens and Clarke County, was originally a residence for workers in the Agricultural Adjustment Administration, but today mainly houses extension service staff members, including offices of the 4-H program.

Hoke Smith was publisher of the *Atlanta Journal* and U.S. secretary of the interior under President Grover Cleveland before being elected governor in 1907 and again in 1910. The General Assembly appointed him in 1911 to fill the seat of an incumbent U.S. senator who had suffered a stroke, and he served until 1921. Closely aligned with the early twentieth-century Progressive movement, Smith, as governor, increased public school funding and established the state board of education. In the Senate, he pushed for passage of the Smith-Lever Act, which established a national agricultural extension system (the Cooperative Extension Service), and the Smith-Hughes Act, which provided for vocational education in secondary schools.

Treanor House

BUILT: ca. 1840s | NAMED FOR: Treanor family | CURRENT USE: Office of the Vice President for Public Service and Outreach | BUILDING 1657

Lurking behind giant magnolia trees, the Treanor House has a somewhat mysterious history. It is believed that the house—or a predecessor—dates to at least the early 1840s, when it may have been built by John Addison Cobb as a wed-

ding gift to his daughter, Laura Cobb Rutherford. It was occupied by members of the Cobb, Rutherford, and Lipscomb families, all prominent in Athens history, and was the birthplace in 1851 of Mildred Rutherford, a noted Athens educator and longtime principal of the Lucy Cobb Institute. In 1912, the house was purchased by Alexander Ashford, a wealthy Watkinsville merchant, as a residence for his four sons while they attended UGA. In 1929, it was purchased by Kate McKinley Treanor, whose family owned it until UGA bought it in 1987. An unusual architectural feature is the Gothic Revival portico. Slim, attenuated columns combine with brackets to form pseudo-arches that divide the porch into seven bays. In 1979, the house was listed on the National Register of Historic Places. Adjacent to the Treanor House is the Cobb House, headquarters of the Office of International Public Service and Outreach.

J. W. Fanning Building

BUILT: 2002 | NAMED FOR: J. W. Fanning, the first UGA vice president for services and a pioneer in community leadership development | CURRENT USE: J. W. Fanning Institute for Leadership Development | BUILDING 1675

J. W. (John William) Fanning is widely considered the father of community development and leadership training in Georgia. He earned bachelor's and master's degrees in agricultural economics from UGA in the 1920s and worked with his alma mater for more than half a century as an extension agent, professor, and administrator. In 1961, he founded the Institute of Community and Area Development, which marshaled UGA's technical expertise and resources to help rural and urban communities throughout Georgia. From 1965 until retiring in 1971, he was the university's first vice president for services, helping build UGA's reputation as a premier public service institution. In 1972, Fanning joined other state leaders to create Leadership Georgia; he was a mentor and consultant for the program until his death in 1997 at the age of ninety-one. Staffers in the Fanning Institute for Leadership Development, created in 1982, advise and assist Georgia communities on matters including health care access, environmental problems, economic development, poverty reduction, comprehensive planning, quality growth, and volunteer cultivation.

Myers Hall

BUILT: 1952 | NAMED FOR: Jennie Belle Myers, a housemother in women's residence halls | CURRENT USE: Student residence hall | BUILDING 1222

Myers Hall was built to complete a quadrangle of women's residence halls that included Soule, Mary Lyndon, and Rutherford. Myers had amenities not found in other dormitories, including a library, sundecks, guest suites, and lounges. In the basement was a combination grill and bookstore named The Jenny Bell, which was fronted by a bell moved from the Coordinate Campus, where many of the building's first occupants had lived. Myers was reserved for women until 1974, when men were allowed to live in one of the building's

I was blessed to have been a student at Georgia during extraordinary times. A Kappa Delta on Milledge Avenue, I heard the buzz around the house one day in 1974 that a big event would happen that night on North Campus. Several sisters and I loaded up and went to watch as a huge crowd gathered in front of the Student Union and hundreds of brave students stripped and ran across the bridge buck naked, taking part in a new craze—streaking. There was even a beautiful girl wearing only long hair, like Lady Godiva, riding a horse, mixed in with the mob. She was rumored to have been planted there as part of a photo shoot by a national magazine. Whatever the case, it was all very exciting, and it did make it into all the networks, newspapers, and Georgia history.

Brenda H. Manley, Class of 1975; MS, 1983; DVM, 1986

wings. Cable modems were first tested in UGA residence halls in Myers in 1998. Today about half the 406 rooms are reserved for Honors Program students, who enjoy enriched academic programs and activities. Charlayne Hunter, UGA's first female African American student, lived in Myers, and the lobby has an exhibit with a timeline, photographs, and memorabilia commemorating UGA's desegregation. Myers Quad, behind the building, is a favorite spot for students to socialize and play Frisbee and football.

On an unseasonably warm night in early March 1974, at the height of the national streaking craze, a crowd of students estimated at more than one thousand—most of them naked—congregated in the Myers Quad. Encouraged by a Godiva-esque young woman astride a white horse, they set out on a mass streak across the Sanford Drive Bridge to Reed Quad. The parade earned UGA the unofficial designation as the site of the nation's largest streak.

Jennie Belle Myers, who earned a bachelor's degree in home economics from UGA in 1927, was the housemother in Soule Hall, the first women's residence hall, and worked for twenty-six years as a housemother. She established a scholarship fund for home economics students, one of the first such funds available to female students.

Mary Lyndon Hall

BUILT: 1936 | NAMED FOR: Mary D. Lyndon, the first woman to earn a UGA degree |
CURRENT USE: Student residence hall | BUILDING 1221

Mary Lyndon Hall was the second residence hall for women. Georgian Revival in style, the building was constructed with PWA funds and represented another early use of steel-frame construction. It was designed to provide an "enhanced living atmosphere" for women; its open fireplaces had marble hearths and were decorated with candlesticks and statuettes. When the university began creating living communities composed of students with common academic interests, Mary Lyndon was set aside for students studying Spanish or French.

The building's namesake, Mary Dorothy Lyndon, was the first woman to earn a degree from UGA. Well before women were admitted as regular students in 1918, the university allowed those who wanted to be teachers to earn academic credits in summer school. Lyndon took advantage of this policy and received a master's degree in education in 1914. She later joined the faculty of the School of Education and became the first dean of women.

Rutherford Hall

BUILT: 1939; rebuilt 2013 | NAMED FOR: Mildred Lewis Rutherford, an Athens educator, historian, and author | CURRENT USE: Student residence hall | BUILDING 1210

The original Rutherford Hall was the third women's residence hall on South Campus and was considered by many to be the most architecturally attractive of all the PWA buildings. Its graceful Colonial Revival style, featuring a gabled roof and stone pillars supporting tall Doric columns, suggested an eighteenth-century plantation house. But seventy-two years of constant use took its toll, and by 2011 the building, which housed 159 students, was beset with many problems, including inadequate drainage, mold, and inaccessible and inefficient utility lines. After a lengthy study of possible options, university officials decided that renovation would be prohibitively costly; the building was razed in 2012. The current building, which opened in 2013 with space for 260 residents, retains the original structure's historic character but complies with modern safety, comfort, and environmental standards.

Mildred "Miss Milly" Rutherford, born in Athens in 1851, was the niece of prominent Athens lawyers Howell and T. R. R. Cobb. She was associated with the Lucy Cobb Institute, a girls' finishing school in Athens, from 1880 until her death in 1928, including twenty-two years as the school's principal. A devoted educator, she instituted a demanding academic curriculum but also taught young girls proper decorum and behavior. A staunch defender of the Old South, she was historian for life of the Georgia Division of the United Daughters of the Confederacy and wrote and spoke extensively about the Civil War era.

Athletic Facilities

The southernmost part of South Campus is home to several Bulldog athletic teams. The men's and women's tennis teams compete in the Dan Magill Tennis Complex, one of the largest and best collegiate tennis venues in the country. Foley Field is one of the top collegiate baseball stadiums. The men's and women's basketball teams and the women's gymnastics team compete in Stegeman Coliseum and practice in the adjacent Coliseum Training Facility. Spec Towns Track is the home of the men's and women's track and field teams, and the football team drills on the Woodruff Practice Fields. Butts-Mehre Heritage Hall includes training, medical, and meeting spaces for the football team and houses a museum that showcases athletic trophies, exhibits, and memorabilia. All these facilities are part of the Vince Dooley Athletic Complex, named for the former football coach and athletic director who is one of the most honored and respected figures in UGA athletic history.

Detailed information on these and other athletic facilities is in chapter 7.

CHAPTER 5 # East Campus

EAST CAMPUS is bounded by East Campus Road on the west, College Station Road on the South, the Athens Perimeter / Loop 10 on the east, and River Road on the north.

After completing a tour of campus on July 1, 1987, his first day as the university's twentieth president, Charles Knapp knew what one of his top priorities would be. Knapp had been particularly appalled by the sad condition of the Fine Arts Building, then home of the Music and Drama Departments, and Stegeman Hall, the main student recreation facility. "I came out of those tours saying, 'Those facilities have got to be replaced,'" Knapp later recalled.

By the time Knapp stepped down ten years later, more than seventy-five acres of rural fields and pastures east of the main campus had been transformed into a spectacular new sector dubbed East Campus. It included not only a mammoth student recreation center and a spacious music building, but also a performing arts center, an art museum, a student health center, and a visitors center—more than six hundred thousand square feet of new space worth nearly $100 million. Subsequent development included major facilities for art education and advanced scientific research, five student residence halls, and a dining facility. With its handsome buildings, state-of-the-art technology, and modern environmental amenities, East Campus blends academic, cultural, and recreational interests in a finely landscaped setting that is a showcase for twenty-first-century educational planning and design.

The campus's anchor building, the enormous Ramsey Student Physical Activities Center, is one of the largest such facilities in the country. The music and art buildings, which house schools named for two Georgia pioneers in music and art education, provide space for some fifteen hundred students to study, train, and practice. The Rhodes Center for Animal and Dairy Science is home to scientists whose research is opening new frontiers in cloning and stem cell therapy.

Many of the internationally renowned artists who appear in the Performing Arts Center proclaim it to be one of the best concert halls in which they have performed. The Georgia Museum of Art is the state's official art museum and houses one of the largest and most valuable art collections in Georgia.

The East Campus Village residence halls, the first new dormitories at UGA in more than three decades, reflect modern attitudes about the housing needs and preferences of students. At the Student Health Center, students can be treated for anything from a bad cold to a broken bone, but they can also get counseling and assistance with handling social and emotional issues.

While East Campus can't match its North, Central, and South Campus counterparts in history and tradition, the area has its own unique feeling—a lively mix of creative energy, academic excellence, visual charm, and bustling student activity.

Performing
Arts Center
1692

School of Music
1691

Georgia
Museum of Art
1693

School of Art
1694

CARLTON STREET

EAST CAMPUS ROAD

RIVER ROAD

Joe Frank Harris
Commons
1511

CARLTON STREET

Busbee Hall
1512

McWhorter Hall
1515

EAST CAMPUS VILLAGE

Vandiver Hall
1514

Rooker Hall
1513

Building
1516

University
Health Center
1701

Visitors Center
(Four Towers
Building)
2835

Rhodes Center
for Animal and
Dairy Science
1501–1503

RIVER ROAD

COLLEGE STATION ROAD

Performing Arts Center

BUILT: 1995 | CURRENT USE: Concert halls for performances by internationally renowned musicians | BUILDING 1692

Hailed as the finest concert venue in Georgia and among the best in the South, the Performing Arts Center gives audiences unforgettable experiences provided by some of the greatest musical performers of our time. The center's main auditorium—eleven-hundred-seat Hodgson Hall—is an acoustic gem with high-tech panels that slide up or down to "tune" the room. Seats are arranged "festival style" to surround the 2,360-foot stage, providing excellent visibility from anywhere in the hall. Internationally famous music stars, symphonic orchestras, and chamber music groups perform in Hodgson Hall, along with a variety of other popular musical, comedy, and entertainment acts. Also in the center is 360-seat Ramsey Hall, a more intimate venue for solo performances by new artists and small chamber groups. Hodgson Hall is named for Hugh Hodgson, the founder of UGA's School of Music, and Ramsey Hall is named for Bernard Ramsey, one of UGA's most generous benefactors.

Georgia Museum of Art

BUILT: 1996, with a major addition in 2011 | CURRENT USE: Georgia Museum of Art | BUILDING 1693

In the early 1940s, the New York lawyer and art collector Alfred Heber Holbrook visited Athens and met Lamar Dodd, the head of the UGA Art Department. A close friendship developed, and in 1945 Holbrook gave UGA one hundred paintings by U.S. artists to start an art museum. He also moved to Athens to be the museum's director. Housed initially in the basement of the university library (in the North Campus building that is now the Administration Building), the tiny museum grew steadily thanks to the guidance and generosity of Holbrook, who served for twenty-five years as director and gave more than nine hundred works to the museum's permanent collection. When the library moved to larger quarters in 1954, the museum expanded into the entire building.

Though designated by the Georgia General Assembly in 1982 as the official state museum of art, the museum could exhibit only a fraction of its works in its cramped space. That problem was alleviated in 1996 with the move to this modern building, originally 52,000 square feet in size. A $20 million expansion completed in 2011 added 29,970 square feet, including 16,000 square feet of

Georgia Museum of Art Holdings

Included in the Georgia Museum of Art's permanent collection are works by major American artists, including Georgia O'Keeffe, Winslow Homer, Stuart Davis, William Merritt Chase, Paul Cadmus, Alice Neel, Elaine de Kooning, and Lamar Dodd. The museum hosts exhibitions from leading international museums such as the Palazzo Venezia in Rome, the Rembrandt House Museum in Amsterdam, and the National Gallery of Scotland.

My husband, Charles, and I were both members of the Georgia Redcoat Band (back then
it was the Dixie Redcoat Band). I saw him the
first day I was at UGA (during band practice),
met him the second day during a band mixer,
dated him all four years that I was at Georgia,
and married him two weeks after I graduated. We have been married for thirty-seven
years, and we have a daughter, Kathryn, who
attended UGA and was also in the Redcoat
Band. Once a Dawg, always a Dawg!

Patricia Kight Cheney, Class of 1975;
MEd, 2005

gallery space, along with an outdoor sculpture garden, an expanded lobby, and more storage space. The expansion received Gold LEED certification for the use of materials and construction strategies to achieve environmental sustainability.

As both an academic museum and a traditional art museum, the Georgia Museum of Art fosters teaching, research, and outreach as well as enjoyment of art. In addition to extensive galleries, the museum has an education suite with classrooms, a library, and a two-hundred-seat auditorium, along with a snack bar and gift shop. The museum's permanent collection of more than eight thousand objects centers on nineteenth- and twentieth-century American paintings. Other holdings include large collections of American, European, and Asian works on paper; Italian Renaissance paintings; Asian art; and southern decorative arts. The museum is home to four specialized centers that use the collections to promote study and research in the humanities: the Henry Green Center for the Study of the Decorative Arts; the Jacob Burns Foundation Center, which is the primary repository for the works of the British artist Gerald Brockhurst; the Pierre Daura Center, with more than six hundred works by the noted Catalan American artist; and the C. L. Morehead Jr. Center for the Study of American Art. Admission to the museum is free. For hours and more information, visit www.georgiamuseum.org.

School of Music

BUILT: 1995 | CURRENT USE: Hugh Hodgson School of Music | BUILDING 1691

Some 450 undergraduate and graduate music majors come to this one-hundred-thousand-square-foot building to study, create, practice, and perform music in all its many forms and formats. The building includes soundproof classrooms, offices, and faculty studios; a black-box multimedia space with a recording booth; and computer labs where students can instantly transform their original compositions into electronic sheet music. A music library contains audio and video recordings, books, scores, and music education materials. Rehearsal spaces were designed for acoustical advantage, with curved and angled walls, slant-pitched ceilings, special acoustical tiles, and sound-muffling curtains and doors. Spaces range in size from

UGA *Alma Mater*

The university was more than a century old before it had a song to serve as the alma mater. The familiar alma mater melody played today at football games and graduation exercises did not come into use until J. B. Wright Jr., a 1914 graduate, wrote words for an old Latin tune, "Amici," that many schools have adopted as their alma mater. Hugh Hodgson, a music professor, arranged the tune for Wright's lyrics. When Wright penned the original three verses and chorus, women had not been admitted to the university as regular students, so all the song's gender references were male. In 1990, in response to complaints that the lyrics were exclusionary because there was no reference to female students, the Alumni Society Board of Managers voted to add a new verse that recognizes the presence of women. Written by Gail Carter Dendy, a native Athenian and UGA alumna (BA, 1974; MA, 1981), the new verse was inserted as the song's third verse. None of Wright's words were eliminated or changed, but today only the first, third, and fourth verses are usually sung. Hodgson's original arrangement was updated by Tom Wallace (BM, 1970; MFA, 1972), longtime arranger for the UGA Redcoat Band. Here are the words to the alma mater.

VERSE 1

From the hills of Georgia's northland
Beams thy noble brow,
And the sons of Georgia rising,
Pledge with sacred vow.

CHORUS

Alma Mater, thee we'll honor
True and loyal be,
Ever crowned with praise and glory,
Georgia, hail to thee.

VERSE 2

'Neath the pine trees' stately shadow
Spread thy riches rare.
And thy sons, dear Alma Mater
Will thy treasures share.

VERSE 3

And thy daughters proudly join thee,
Take their rightful place.
Side by side into the future,
Equal dreams embrace.

VERSE 4

Through the ages, Alma Mater,
Men will look to thee.
Thou the fairest of the Southland,
Georgia's Varsity.

Hugh Hodgson and orchestra

rooms large enough to hold the four-hundred-member Redcoat Band to more than fifty small modular rooms for individual practice. The music school supports several faculty ensembles and more than thirty student groups: large concert bands, symphonic bands, choirs, smaller jazz bands, and ensembles for opera, brass, trumpet, percussion, African American music, and chamber music. The groups annually perform more than three hundred concerts and recitals, many in the 180-seat Edge Recital Hall, named for Robert Edge, a UGA alumnus and arts patron from Atlanta.

The music school was named in 2005 for the Athens native and 1915 UGA graduate Hugh Hodgson, whose appointment as music professor in 1928 is considered the start of the university's music program. Hodgson developed four degree programs in music, including the first graduate degree, and was the first chairman of the Division of Fine Arts. He conducted student choral and symphonic groups, helped establish the Atlanta and Savannah symphony orchestras, and arranged and wrote the words for UGA's famous fight song, "Glory, Glory to Old Georgia."

School of Art

BUILT: 2008 | CURRENT USE: Lamar Dodd School of Art | BUILDING 1694

The arrival of the Lamar Dodd School of Art on East Campus from North Campus was the last step in fulfilling a long-standing vision of bringing together two signature components of UGA's fine arts program—the schools of music and art. From humble beginnings in the 1920s, when home economics offered classes in drawing and design, the art school has flourished, attaining national stature, an undergraduate enrollment of one thousand, and lofty rankings for its graduate programs. With this $40 million, 120,000-square-foot building, which is marked by airy, open spaces, specialized facilities, and advanced environmental features, the school is also one of the finest in the country for teaching and creative expression in the visual arts.

The building includes classrooms and dedicated studios for painting and drawing, fabric design, printmaking and book arts, graphic design, scientific illustration, art education, digital media, and photography. There are galleries, wood and metal shops, and multimedia lecture halls for instruction in art history and art education. The building features advanced green-building technologies, including the use of indigenous and recycled materials,

Lamar Dodd

Lamar Dodd with students

The location of the art building next to the School of Music symbolically recalls that it was Hugh Hodgson, founder of the music school, who brought Lamar Dodd to the UGA Art Department in 1937. The next year, Dodd, a native of Fairburn, Georgia, was appointed department head and became one of the South's pioneering art educators and leading artists. He directed the Art Department (later School) until 1973, building it into one of the nation's leading collegiate art-education programs. He was also chair of the Division of Fine Arts for sixteen years and served on the U.S. Advisory Committee on the Arts. Dodd was a nationally acclaimed artist who employed styles ranging from realism to abstraction to create hundreds of paintings and drawings, including still lifes, portraits, landscapes, and sports scenes. Among his best-known works are a series of colorful paintings created for NASA in the 1960s and 1970s depicting space shots, and dramatic portrayals of the drama of heart surgery. He received scores of prizes for his paintings, which were shown in more than one hundred one-man exhibitions and are in many private collections and major museums, including the Whitney Museum of American Art in New York, the Metropolitan Museum of Art, the High Museum of Art in Atlanta, and the National Gallery of Art in Washington, D.C. The Dodd School created a professorial chair and a scholarship in his name.

water-efficient fixtures, and a green roof. Energy costs are lowered by the use of natural light, lighting sensors, solar shades and light shelves, and a heat-recovery system. A thirty-five-thousand-gallon underground cistern captures rain and condensate water for reuse in landscape irrigation.

Joe Frank Harris Commons

BUILT: 2004 | NAMED FOR: Joe Frank Harris, Georgia governor, 1983–91 |
CURRENT USE: Student dining facility | BUILDING 1511

Constructed as part of East Campus Village, this fifty-two-thousand-square-foot building is a hub of student activities on East Campus. A dramatic stair-case leads to the second-floor Village Summit, a five-hundred-seat dining hall with sweeping views of the surrounding landscape. Open seven days a week,

the Summit has specialty stations offering hot entrees and vegetables; made-to-order pizzas, omelets, deli and grilled sandwiches, and salads; vegetarian cuisine; smoothies, ice cream, yogurt, and desserts; and hot and cold beverages. The smaller Red Clay Café includes a coffee shop with gourmet coffee, pastries, ice cream, and desserts; a sandwich shop featuring freshly baked bread and soups; and a salad shop with a wide array of freshly chopped ingredients. The Village Market sells snacks, candy, salads, sandwiches, bottled and canned beverages, and some school supplies and personal grooming items. The building has spaces for meetings and student activities also. In addition, the building contains a commissary and the production facilities to support three other large student dining halls and six other eateries operated by University Food Services at other campus locations. Under the slogan "Where the Big Dawg Eats," University Food Services serves thousands of students daily and has won more than seventy-five national awards for excellence and innovation in quality and customer service.

Joe Frank Harris, a native of Cartersville, Georgia, earned a business degree from UGA in 1958 and served for eighteen years in the Georgia House of Representatives before being elected governor. He instituted the Quality Basic Education program, created the Georgia Research Consortium, and boosted state funding for education by $2 billion. When his term ended, Harris became the first former governor appointed to the University System Board of Regents.

University Health Center

BUILT: 1997, enlarged in 2009 | CURRENT USE: Comprehensive health care
for students | BUILDING 1701

Whether it is a headache or a sprained ankle, anxiety attacks or the flu, the
University Health Center is where students go when they are sick or injured
or need advice or information on health matters. The staff of two hundred
represents twenty health professions and includes board-certified physicians,
registered nurses, psychologists, physical therapists, medical and radiologic
technologists, counselors, and health educators. The center includes an urgent
care clinic and triage center, a medical laboratory, a radiology department, a
physical therapy department, a pharmacy, and rooms for minor surgery. There
are specialized clinics for women's health; dental, vision, and allergy problems;
and sleep disorders. The center provides massage therapy, dermatology con-
sultations, and counseling on mental health, stress management, substance
abuse, sexual health, and diet or nutrition. A sports medicine and physical
therapy clinic diagnoses and treats nonsurgical orthopedic problems for athletes and nonathletes. Students can get advice and vaccinations for international travel as well as flu shots and immunizations. The health center has
earned Accreditation with Commendation, the highest recognition from the
Joint Commission on Accreditation of Healthcare Organizations, and frequently is cited as a benchmark of exemplary comprehensive campus health
services.

Since it opened in 1996, the Visitors Center has logged more than 792,000 visitor contacts. This includes more than 235,000 walk-in guests and more than 265,900 telephone contacts. The center has provided individual or group tours for more than 186,300 participants.

Visitors Center (Four Towers Building)

BUILT: 1940 | CURRENT USE: Welcomes campus visitors, provides information about UGA, and offers campus tours | BUILDING 2835

When UGA was chosen to host soccer, volleyball, and rhythmic gymnastics competitions for the 1996 Atlanta Olympics, officials converted a portion of a former agricultural barn into a welcome center for the expected throngs of spectators. With engaging interactive displays, colorful campus photos and exhibits, and a friendly and eager student staff, the center was an instant success. Today the static displays and exhibits have given way to video screens and computers, but the student staff still warmly greets some forty thousand prospective students, tourists, alumni, sports fans, and other visitors each year. The staff also handles about fifteen thousand telephone calls and e-mails annually. The Visitors Center shares the building—known as Four Towers for its four distinctive silos—with units of the College of Agricultural and Environmental Sciences. The original building, initially a dairy barn and later

a poultry research facility, opened in 1940 as one of the smaller projects paid for with PWA funding; two wings were later added on each side. In addition to greeting visitors, answering questions, and providing information about UGA, the Visitors Center student staff leads daily driving and walking tours of campus. The students—selected competitively through interviews—are especially helpful in giving prospective students personal insights on every aspect of student life at UGA. Tours can be arranged by calling 706-542-0842 or through the online reservation system at www.visit.uga.edu.

East Campus Village

BUILT: 2004 | CURRENT USE: Student housing | BUILDING 1512 (Busbee Hall) | BUILDING 1513 (Rooker Hall) | BUILDING 1514 (Vandiver Hall) | BUILDING 1515 (McWhorter Hall) | BUILDING 1516

The four buildings of the seven-acre East Campus Village provide accommodations and amenities to meet the independent living needs of today's college students. Home to more than twelve hundred students—mostly upperclassmen, graduate students, and athletes—the buildings were the first new residence halls constructed at UGA in more than thirty years. Each building has apartment-style suites with fully furnished private bedrooms and a living room; a private or semiprivate bathroom; and kitchen areas with a sink, counter stools, a microwave, and a refrigerator. Each suite has telephone and cable television connections and high-speed Internet service. The buildings have meeting and study rooms, computer labs, a multipurpose room with a kitchen, laundry facilities, and a twenty-four-hour service desk. Admission to the residential areas of the buildings is through a hand-reader access system. The fire alarm and sprinkler system is linked directly to UGA police.

Rooker Hall is named for the Atlanta real estate and construction executive John W. (Jack) Rooker, a 1960 graduate and generous financial supporter who was chairman of both the University of Georgia Foundation and the UGA Real Estate Foundation. Rooker Hall's spacious student commons area, featuring a large stone fireplace, is named the Cynthia W. (Cindy) Rooker Fireside Lounge in honor of Rooker's wife, a 1962 graduate.

Vandiver Hall is named for Ernest Vandiver, who earned business and law degrees at UGA and served as governor of Georgia from 1959 to 1963. Vandiver increased state funding for higher education and supported major construction projects at UGA but may best be remembered for his leadership in refusing to close the university when federal courts ordered racial integration in 1961.

The crisp fall air of football season and game time. The deafening sounds of the best band in the SEC, playing anthems which we Dawgs took so much pride in. Memories of football seasons in Athens, Georgia, are truly magical to alumni and fans alike. My favorite memory of football season was when I first arrived as a freshman at the University of Georgia in 2007. I had been moved from Brumby Hall to East Campus Village in early September of freshman year, and was happily coming home one evening when I encountered Matthew Stafford, the sophomore quarterback whom I had always admired as a football player, outside our building. He politely held the door for me to enter the building, and all I could think was, "Wow! The best arm in the nation is holding the door for me, a lowly freshman, right now!" A couple months later, it was wonderful to see that arm beat Auburn 45–20 in the Georgia-Auburn "Blackout" game while all my new friends cheered on the team that had become a part of us. I knew I had picked the right place to call home. Truly magical.

Megan Kelley, Class of 2011

McWhorter Hall is named for Bob McWhorter Sr., a football star in the early twentieth century who was UGA's first all-American and the first UGA player enshrined in the National Football Hall of Fame. After graduation, McWhorter earned a law degree at the University of Virginia and then returned to Athens to teach in the UGA law school for thirty-five years and serve four terms as the city's mayor.

Busbee Hall is named for George D. Busbee, who earned bachelor's and law degrees at UGA and served as Georgia's seventy-seventh governor from 1975 to 1983.

In 2010, a fifth residence hall (Building 1516) opened adjacent to East Campus Village. This building, which houses about five hundred students, has traditional double and single rooms rather than apartments. It is part of the community of residence halls that includes Reed and Payne in Central Campus and Morris Hall in North Campus. Reflecting the university's commitment to sustainable development, the building was the first residence hall to earn Gold LEED certification from the U.S. Green Building Council for such eco-friendly construction features as the use of energy-efficient windows, plumbing, appliances, and HVAC systems; Forest Stewardship Council–certified wood; high-value insulation; carpet, paint, and adhesives with low-volatile organic compounds; and separate storage tanks to catch and treat rain and condensate water and grey water from showers and laundry.

Rhodes Center for Animal and Dairy Science

BUILT: 1998 | NAMED FOR: Edgar L. Rhodes, former chairman of the University System
Board of Regents | CURRENT USE: Animal and Dairy Science Department | BUILDINGS 1501,
1502, 1503

This three-building complex, encompassing 135,000 square feet, is one of the
nation's most advanced facilities for research to improve the productivity
and economic value of dairy and beef cattle, swine, and
horses. The Animal and Dairy Science Department, part of
the College of Agricultural and Environmental Sciences,
focuses on research in biotechnology, genetics, animal
nutrition, and animal physiology. Scientists in the center
have earned international reputations for breakthroughs
in cloning technology and related stem cell therapy. Other
research focuses on genetic advances in cattle breeding;
improvements in the health and safety of red meat products; the creation of more affordable and environmentally friendly management plans for livestock produc-
ers; and the preservation and development of grasslands
and forage areas. The center's classrooms are equipped to
train students in both the agribusiness and production
segments of animal agriculture. The Animal and Dairy
Science Department conducts an extensive outreach program through 4-H and Future Farmers of America as a
way to teach and train young Georgians about livestock
production.

Edgar Rhodes, a 1938 graduate of UGA's agricultural college, was a prominent businessman and farmer in Bremen,
Georgia, and a leading advocate for agricultural educa-
tion in the state. He was instrumental in helping UGA obtain state funding for
the animal and dairy science center, and he created a scholarship endowment
for students studying animal and dairy science. Rhodes served on the board
of regents from 1984 to 1999 and was chair from 1989 to 1991. He also served
on the State Board of Technical and Adult Education and was elected to the
Georgia Agricultural Hall of Fame.

CHAPTER 6   Off Campus

IN ADDITION TO THE 759 acres of the main campus, the university owns several thousand additional acres in Clarke and neighboring Oconee, Oglethorpe, Madison, and Jackson Counties. Much of this is farmland and forestland used for teaching and research in agriculture, animal science, forestry, ecology, and veterinary medicine. Additionally, UGA owns some thirty-three thousand acres in other locations, ranging from the North Georgia mountains to the Atlantic Coast. Most of this property is also for research and education in science-related areas, though it includes several 4-H centers, an Indian mound complex in Stewart County, a bamboo farm in Chatham County, and marshlands in Camden County.

About much of the off-campus land in Clarke County was acquired through purchase or by donation from private owners, and much of it is historically significant to Athens. The university has been careful to preserve and improve these structures and spaces. Some of the Clarke County land is immediately west of the main campus in an emerging Northwest Quadrant that includes one of the university's oldest buildings—the Wray-Nicholson House, built in 1825—and one of its newest—the Richard B. Russell Building Special Collections Libraries, opened in 2012. The area also includes a cluster of residence halls built in the 1960s. Construction is underway at the intersection of Baxter and Lumpkin Streets on a $45 million building for the Terry College of Business—the first in a planned complex of new facilities for the growing college.

About three miles south of campus is the State Botanical Garden of Georgia, a 313-acre forest and wildlife preserve that is both a popular tourist attraction and an important resource for research and education in ecology and the natural sciences. About two miles northwest of campus is the Health Sciences Campus, a fifty-six-acre complex where UGA and Georgia Regents University are working to improve the health of Georgians by training new physicians and finding new ways to treat and prevent diseases and medical problems that plague the state. About a mile southeast of campus is the Riverbend Research Site, which features a cluster of specialized science facilities.

Other off-campus sites include three structures with histories that extend deep into Athens's past: the Lucy Cobb Institute, a former nineteenth-century girls' school now occupied by the Carl Vinson Institute of Government; the President's Home, with its extensive collection of antique furnishings; and White Hall, a secluded mansion noted for its curious architectural style.

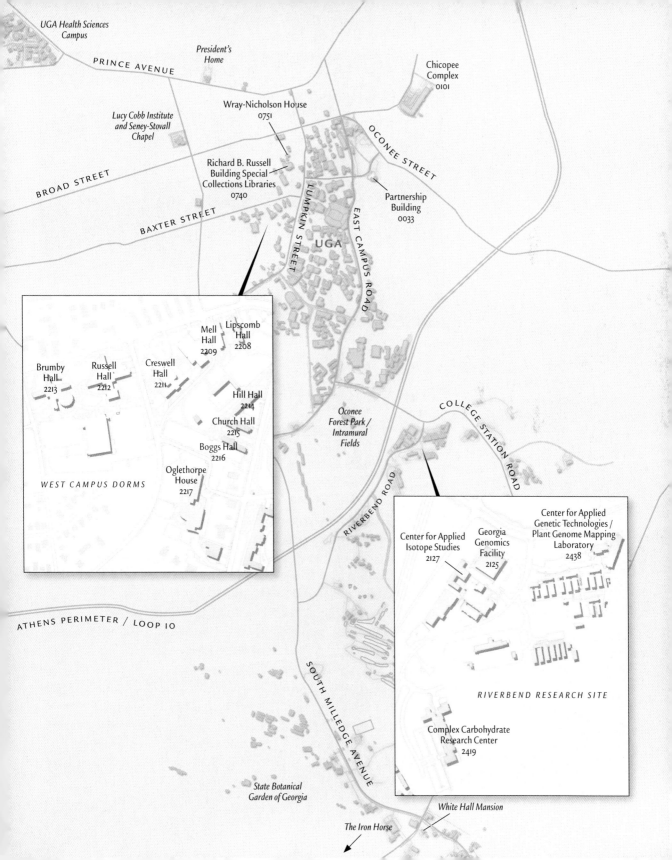

UGA Health Sciences
Campus

PRINCE AVENUE

President's
Home

Chicopee
Complex
0101

Wray-Nicholson House
0751

Lucy Cobb Institute
and Seney-Stovall
Chapel

OCONEE STREET

BROAD STREET

Richard B. Russell
Building Special
Collections Libraries
0740

BAXTER STREET

LUMPKIN STREET

EAST CAMPUS ROAD

Partnership
Building
0033

UGA

Mell
Hall
2209

Lipscomb
Hall
2208

Brumby
Hall
2213

Russell
Hall
2212

Creswell
Hall
2211

Hill Hall
2214

Church Hall
2215

Boggs Hall
2216

Oglethorpe
House
2217

WEST CAMPUS DORMS

Oconee
Forest Park /
Intramural
Fields

COLLEGE STATION ROAD

ATHENS PERIMETER / LOOP 10

RIVERBEND ROAD

Center for Applied
Isotope Studies
2127

Georgia
Genomics
Facility
2125

Center for Applied
Genetic Technologies /
Plant Genome Mapping
Laboratory
2438

RIVERBEND RESEARCH SITE

SOUTH MILLEDGE AVENUE

Complex Carbohydrate
Research Center
2419

State Botanical
Garden of Georgia

White Hall Mansion

The Iron Horse

Popular UGA Songs

A version of UGA's best-known fight song, "Glory, Glory," was sung as early as the 1890s, but became popular after the music professor Hugh Hodgson created a jaunty arrangement to the tune of the chorus of "The Battle Hymn of the Republic." The song's popularity stems from the melody and not the words, which are decidedly unimaginative:

> Glory, Glory to Old Georgia
>
> Glory, Glory to Old Georgia
>
> Glory, Glory to Old Georgia
>
> G-E-O-R-G-I-A

Hodgson arranged other "pep" songs that emerged in the early twentieth century, including "I Want To Go Back" and "Bulldog Marching Song." He collaborated with his cousin, Morton Hodgson, a 1909 graduate, on the popular "Going Back (to Athens Town)," and Morton wrote and arranged a song titled "Oh! We'll Whoop 'Em Up for U-G-A." A song by Ernest Rogers titled "She's the Daughter of the Red and Black" brought cheers with the lines "Can't hold herself in check when she yells 'to hell with Tech.'" Gaines Walter, a Redcoat Band member from 1912 to 1917, wrote words and music for "Hail to Georgia (Down in Dixie)" and "Here Comes the Bulldog." Most of the old songs were part of the Redcoat Band's repertoire for many years, but were played less often in recent years until 2012, when the band revived "Hail to Georgia" in its football pregame show. The Glee Club performs some of the old songs as part of its popular "Bulldog Medley."

Wray-Nicholson House

BUILT: 1825 | NAMED FOR: Thomas Wray and John Nicholson | LOCATION: 298 Hull Street | CURRENT USE: UGA Alumni Association | BUILDING 0751

Located in one of the oldest neighborhoods in Athens, this imposing Greek Revival mansion has been enlarged and upgraded a number of times since the university erected it on the edge of campus as a dining hall for students. Thomas Wray, a cotton merchant, bought it in 1845 as a private residence and made significant architectural improvements. He sold it in 1867 to John Nicholson, a businessman who made further additions, including installing two-tiered porches. In 1916, the porches were replaced by the present portico, which has six tall Doric columns relocated from an antebellum mansion on Prince Avenue. Nicholson's daughter-in-law, Lucy Woodall Nicholson, was an avid gardener who landscaped the grounds with flowers, shrubs, and plants brought from Japan by Commodore Matthew Perry.

In 1964, the family sold the house to a private religious college with the understanding it would be maintained. But in 1994, the college, which had earlier razed an adjacent 1842 house, slated this structure for demolition. Outcries from historic preservationists spurred the Athens–Clarke County government to buy the building and include it in a local-option sales tax referendum that provided $4.4 million for extensive restoration. The government later declared the area a local historic district in order to protect other buildings. In 2000, UGA bought the building, which has about fourteen thousand square feet of office space, to serve as headquarters for the Alumni Association. The house is open to the public.

Richard B. Russell Building Special Collections Libraries

BUILT: 2012 | NAMED FOR: Richard B. Russell, Georgia governor (1930–33), U.S. senator (1933–71) | LOCATION: 300 South Hull Street | CURRENT USE: Three major collections of historical material, UGA Archives | BUILDING 0740

Rare books and maps, historic television and radio shows, and personal files of leading politicians: the contents of the three collections in this building contain some of Georgia's priceless treasures. Formerly stuffed into small spaces in the university's Main Library, the Hargrett Rare Book and Manuscript Library, the Walter J. Brown Media Archive and Peabody Awards, and the Richard B. Russell Library for Political Research and Studies each now has its own spacious, museum-like gallery in this 115,000-square-foot building. Each gallery includes numerous static and interactive exhibits of documents, artifacts, photographs, and other materials, much of which previously could not be publicly displayed because of lack of space.

The size and breadth of each collection is incomparable in Georgia. The Hargrett Library contains 120,000 rare and small-press books and broadsides; six million original documents and images concerning Georgia and other topics; the largest collection in existence of books on Georgia and by Georgians; and fifteen hundred rare maps and other documents pertaining to Georgia's founding as well as its land, plants, and animals. The Brown Media Archive, with more than two hundred thousand titles, is the third largest in the nation, and the Peabody Collection includes more than ninety thousand radio and television shows, representing seventy years of Peabody Award–winning radio, television, cable, and Internet programming. The Russell Library has the second-largest collection of modern congressional materials in the country, along with more than three hundred other collections of material from Georgia governors, senators, state officials, political activists, and commentators, covering more than a century of politics and policymaking.

A highlight of the Russell Library is a ten-foot-by-thirty-six-foot mural painted by the UGA art professor and noted folk artist Art Rosenbaum, and depicting Georgia history from 1906 to the present. The building, which

Study Abroad

A UGA student can study continental ecology in Antarctica, global agriculture and trade in China, or Islamic culture in Morocco. Students can go to Botswana to learn about wildlife conservation, travel to Germany to study health promotion, or take a course on interracial communication in Costa Rica. Responding to the rise of internationalization as a major political and economic force, UGA has made global learning a top priority. Each year, Study Abroad Program participants travel to some seventy countries to take courses taught by UGA faculty on more than one hundred topics. Along with learning about life and culture in other lands, they earn academic credit for the courses, which range in length from ten days to a full semester.

Overall, more than 25 percent of students study in another country before they graduate, surpassing a goal set by Michael Adams when he became president and ranking UGA among the national leaders in study-abroad participation. In addition to study abroad, many students take part in year-long exchange programs with foreign universities or go abroad for internships or research programs arranged by UGA professors. The Study Abroad Program started in 1970 when the Art Department began offering a summer course in the Italian hill town of Cortona. Today, UGA conducts year-round residential programs at facilities it owns in Cortona; Oxford, England; and Costa Rica.

Unique Historical Documents

Among holdings in the Hargrett Rare Books and Manuscript Library are unique documents from two defining moments in Georgia and U.S. history—the original Charter of the University of Georgia, and the original permanent Constitution of the Confederate States of America. Both documents have survived near destruction and are so fragile they can be publicly displayed only one day each year.

The UGA Charter has been termed one of the most significant documents in U.S. history because it gave birth to the first institution of higher education in the country established by a state government. The charter's enlightened view that education is the right of all citizens and an obligation of government set the stage for the creation of the U.S. system of public colleges and universities. Drafted primarily by Abraham Baldwin, the charter—written in ink on two sheets of vellum 19.5 by 32.5 inches long—was adopted by the Georgia General Assembly on January 27, 1785, in Savannah. It traveled, apparently unprotected, with files of state documents as Georgia's capital moved to Augusta, Louisville, Milledgeville, and finally Atlanta. Legend has it that a custodian rescued the soiled and crum-

The University of Georgia Charter, 1785

pled charter from a pile of papers about to be burned at the state capitol and took it to the Georgia secretary of state, who sent it to UGA around 1920. The charter is displayed in the Hargrett Library when UGA celebrates Founders Day on January 27.

Delegates from southern states that seceded from the Union met in Montgomery, Alabama, in early 1861 to adopt a constitution for the Confederate States of America. Thomas R. R. Cobb, an 1841 UGA graduate and prominent Athens lawyer, was the chief author of both a provisional constitution approved on February 4 and a permanent constitution adopted on March 11. Both documents were sent to the Confederate capital in Richmond, Virginia. When Richmond was evacuated in 1865, fleeing Confederate troops carried away the two constitutions along with other Confederate governmental records, but abandoned them at a railroad station in Chester, South Carolina. A newspaper war correspondent, Felix G. DeFontaine, found the constitutions while scavenging for scrap paper. He sold the provisional constitution at auction in New York in 1883, and it is in the Museum of the Confederacy in Richmond. That same year he sold the permanent constitution to Mrs. George Wymberley Jones DeRenne of Savannah, whose family owned a large collection of material related to Georgia. UGA bought the entire DeRenne collection, including the Confederate constitution, in 1939, and that collection formed the nucleus of the Hargrett Library. The handwritten constitution, which fills five vellum sheets pasted together into a roll almost twelve feet long, is stored in a lead-lined cylinder to prevent exposure to light and air. It is displayed on one day each year in conjunction with Confederate Memorial Day, April 26.

received Gold LEED certification for energy efficiency and environmental features, has integrated security and customized climate control, and includes
classrooms, seminar rooms, and a multipurpose room for events. Though the
building appears large and imposing, much of it is not visible. Beneath the
brick structure is a thirty-thousand-square-foot underground vault with rows
of thirty-foot-high shelves. The vault's 220,000 cubic feet can hold some five
million books and thousands of boxes of archival material.

About a third of the building's $46 million cost came from private dona-
tions, including a $3 million lead gift from the Richard B. Russell Foundation.
Russell, a native of Winder, Georgia, earned a law degree from UGA in 1918.
After serving ten years in the Georgia House of Representatives, he was elected
governor. He engineered a massive reorganization of state government that
included the creation of the University System of Georgia. As a U.S. senator
for thirty-eight years, Russell chaired the Senate Appropriations Committee
and the Senate Armed Services Committee and wrote the law that created
the national school lunch program. Namesake of the oldest U.S. Senate office
building, Russell was an adviser to six U.S. presidents and president pro tem of
the Senate, making him third in line of presidential succession, and was himself a candidate for president in 1952.

Georgia Writers
Hall of Fame

The UGA libraries established the Georgia
Writers Hall of Fame in 2000 to recognize
authors for their contributions to the state's
rich literary heritage. Located in the Richard
B. Russell Building Special Collections
Libraries, the hall of fame honors more than
forty writers whose work spans the gamut
of literary forms: fiction, poetry, scholarly
research, popular media, and social and
political commentary. Among the members
are Margaret Mitchell, Martin Luther King Jr.,
Flannery O'Conner, W. E. B. Du Bois, Jimmy
Carter, Pat Conroy, Lillian Smith, Ralph
McGill, Natasha Trethewey, and Terry Kay.

West Campus Dorms

I was the dorm president for Church Hall the last year that there were curfews in place for female students. There was a scare up the hill at the big dorms—we all thought that it was a fire in one of the dorms (Brumby or Creswell). It was right after MLK Jr's assassination, and tensions were high on campus.

Guys from all over town heard the alert and rushed to campus to help. Turned out it was just a problem with steam—comedy ensued. I saw a guy snatch the dean's hat and take off with it.

People were going into their neighbor's rooms and taking undies to throw out the windows. Of course, moms had sewn nametags into the garments. We did not have phones in our rooms at that time, just on the floors. Bras and undies were hung on the boys' dorm bulletin boards for a long time. Many girls got calls who had no idea that their undies had gone out of the windows.

Good clean fun. We made the record books and no one got hurt! It could never happen again.

Ah, the 60s, when sex, drugs, and rock and roll were still harmless.

M. F. Cleveland, Class of 1971

As the first wave of post–World War II baby boomers hit college age and Americans increasingly recognized the economic value of a college degree, UGA's enrollment swelled in the early 1960s, topping ten thousand for the first time in the 1962–63 school year. To house the flood of students, the university used federal urban renewal funds to buy fifty-one acres along the western edge of campus from the city of Athens and to construct eight residence halls and a dining hall. A ninth dorm (Tucker Hall) was built on East Campus Road, primarily to accommodate agricultural students. These dormitories, collectively housing almost four thousand students, reflected a significant shift in both the appearance and the philosophy of student residence halls. Modern and architecturally plain in design, the buildings included three high-rise dorms, each accommodating almost a thousand students, and were grouped into "colonies" to promote cohesiveness and social interaction among students. Unlike earlier spartan dorms that were made up of little more than rows of small rooms, the new facilities included such amenities as lounges, meeting rooms, recreational and study areas, elevators, and air-conditioning. Over time, staffing patterns changed: traditional housemothers were replaced by resident assistants, graduate assistants, hall directors, and professional programming coordinators. Today, some dorms host "learning communities" composed of students with common academic interests, and resident faculty members coordinate in-house academic programs. In 2004, the university adopted a policy requiring freshmen to live on campus. In total, about 5,300 students live in residence halls.

The West Campus dorms and their namesakes are as follows:

Lipscomb Hall (Building 2208): Andrew Lipscomb, UGA chancellor, 1860–74
Mell Hall (Building 2209): Patrick H. Mell, UGA chancellor, 1878–88
Creswell Hall (Building 2211): Mary Creswell, the first female to earn a bachelor's degree at UGA and first dean of the School of Home Economics
Russell Hall (Building 2212): Georgia senator Richard B. Russell
Brumby Hall (Building 2213): Anne W. Brumby, the second dean of women
Hill Hall (Building 2214): Walter B. Hill, UGA chancellor, 1899–1905
Church Hall (Building 2215): Alonzo Church, UGA president, 1829–59
Boggs Hall: (Building 2216): William E. Boggs, UGA chancellor, 1889–99

Another West Campus dorm, Oglethorpe House (Building 2217), was a privately operated residence hall from 1965 until UGA bought it in 1979. It is named for General James Oglethorpe, founder of the colony of Georgia.

Partnership Building

BUILT: 1857 | CURRENT USE: Administrative offices, science classrooms | BUILDING 0033

This spot on the bank of the North Oconee River, originally known as Cedar Shoals, was the site of a series of mills beginning in the late eighteenth century, when the area was on the edge of Indian territory. One of the mill owners was Daniel Easley, who in 1801 sold 633 acres of nearby upland forest to the committee searching for a location for UGA—land that would become North Campus. The area continued as a mill site after the university began and the town of Athens grew up around it. Around 1858, two three-story brick buildings were connected to create this 36,845-square-foot structure to house the Athens Cotton and Wool Factory. Turbines located in an arch-like opening beneath the deck overlooking the river provided power for the building. The factory closed in 1926, and the building served many purposes over the years. Many alumni may remember it as O'Malley's, a popular nightclub and restaurant complex that operated through the 1980s. Later it was a fitness center and then a call center.

UGA *Memory*

To ask an alum of the University of Georgia who had as rich an experience as I did as a student in Athens to come up with a favorite memory would be like asking a New York Yankees fan about a favorite victory. Quite frankly, they are too numerous to count. However, if I had to pick one that puts a smile on my face every time I reminisce, I would have to pick the pledge cleanup "parties" the Friday before every football game in the fall of 1989. I pledged Sigma Nu that fall, and these gatherings on River Road not only got the house ready for the visitors the next day but also allowed us to see a side of the intimidating brothers that caused us to want to be a part of such a special brotherhood. There was plenty of work involved, but while you are mopping the hardwood floors, you are talking to your fellow pledges about who is taking what girl to the game tomorrow or do the Dawgs have an injured player that we need to worry about or what band is playing tomorrow night? Then, when the work is over, the same brothers who were so tough to deal with during the week let their guard down and treat you like part of the fraternity. If I could go back in time and relive any part of my undergrad years in Athens, those fall Fridays before games in 1989 would have to be included.

N. Todd Evans, Class of 1993; MBA, 2011

In 2008, the UGA Real Estate Foundation bought the building and five acres of land. Extensively renovated, the building temporarily housed offices, classrooms, and laboratories for the UGA/Georgia Regents University Medical Partnership while the former Navy Supply Corps School on Prince Avenue was being converted into the Health Sciences Campus. The renovation included preserving many of the building's historic features, including all 127 windows, original beams, oak and maple flooring, and exposed handmade bricks. After the medical partnership moved to its new quarters in 2012, some of the laboratories were turned into science labs and classrooms for UGA students, and other parts of the building became offices. The building is listed on the National Register of Historic Places.

Oconee Forest Park / Intramural Fields

LOCATION: College Station Road, south of East Campus

This sixty-acre forest, with stands of hundred-year-old oak and hickory trees, is all that remains of an extensive old-growth forest that once covered much of the area south of East Campus. During the Depression, the Civilian Conservation Corps used some of the land as a seedling nursery, and professors have long brought students here for teaching and research in botany, ecology, and horticulture. As roads and buildings sprang up in the area in the late 1960s, faculty members in the Warnell School of Forestry and Natural Resources began planning to preserve the remaining woodlands, and in 1982 the school established the Oconee Forest Park as a recreation and education resource for the university and the Athens community.

More than fifty thousand people visit the park annually to exercise, fish, and enjoy the natural surroundings. The 1.5 miles of hiking trails include a Tree Trail with markers identifying many trees. The park also has a 1.2-mile mountain bike trail, a 2.57-mile fitness course with workout stops, an off-leash area for dogs, picnic tables, and landscaped areas with native plants and wildflowers. An interpretive kiosk provides information about the park's history and the plants, animals, and ecology of the forest. The fifteen-acre Lake Allyn Herrick, named for a former forestry school dean, is open for fishing to the university faculty, staff, and students. The bridge and boardwalk over the lake are a memorial to Eugenia Calhoun Hargreaves, the wife of another former forestry dean, Leon A. Hargreaves. The park is open free to the public.

Adjacent to Oconee Forest Park are the Intramural Fields, where student teams compete in softball, flag football, soccer, lacrosse, tennis, and other sports. Intramural competition is managed by the Recreational Sports Department in the Division of Student Affairs.

Riverbend Research Site

LOCATION: Riverbend Road, off College Station Road

Several facilities devoted to highly specialized research in plant and animal genetics, genomics sequencing, carbohydrate science, and isotope studies are located at the Riverbend Research Site, about a mile southeast of campus. Most of the scientists who work in these facilities have faculty appointments in university science departments.

The largest Riverbend facility is the internationally known Complex Carbohydrate Research Center (Building 2419). Some two hundred scientists in this 140,000-square-foot building conduct advanced research on the role of complex carbohydrates in regulating growth, cellular communication, gene expression, immunology, and disease defense in microbes, plants, and animals. The $41 million building, opened in 2004, is the third expansion of the CCRC since it moved to UGA in 1985 from Colorado. As a Georgia Research

Alliance-supported regional center for nuclear magnetic resonance spectroscopy, the center has 300-, 500-, and 600-megaherz NMR spectrometers and was one of the first in the world to receive a powerful 900-megaherz NMR spectrometer for biomolecular studies of liquids and solids. The building includes incubators, fermentation and cell culture rooms, and specialized laboratories and equipment for medical glycoscience research and studies on plant growth, plant bioenergy, and synthetic carbohydrate chemistry. The CCRC, which annually brings in some $10 million in research funds, is home to the Georgia Cancer Center and four federally designated centers for carbohydrate research.

The Center for Applied Genetic Technologies (Building 2438) and its affiliated Plant Genome Mapping Laboratory support genomics research on plants and animals that is important to Georgia agriculture. Scientists work on determining the genetic sequences of plants and animals and develop techniques to allow plants to be genetically engineered. The center houses the Georgia BioBusiness Center, which provides management assistance and other resources for bioscience start-up companies.

Other facilities at the Riverbend Research Site include the Georgia Genomics Facility (Building 2125), which provides gene sequencing and genotyping services; the Center for Applied Isotope Studies (Building 2127), which is devoted to research and technical training related to radioisotope and stable isotope nuclear analytical technology; and two buildings that house the Georgia Museum of Natural History's archaeology collection. Offices of the university's Environmental Safety Division are also located at the Riverbend site.

Lucy Cobb Institute and Seney-Stovall Chapel

BUILT: Lucy Cobb Institute, 1858; Seney-Stovall Chapel, 1882 | NAMED FOR: Lucy Cobb, the daughter of the prominent Athenians T. R. R. and Marion Lumpkin Cobb; George Seney and Nellie Stovall. | LOCATION: 201 North Milledge Avenue | CURRENT USE: The Lucy Cobb Institute houses the Carl Vinson Institute of Government; the Seney-Stovall Chapel is a venue for university and community events.

Though there were a dozen or more grammar and high schools in and around Clarke County in the mid-nineteenth century, many families felt that local education was inferior to that offered in the North. In 1854, an Athens mother sent an anonymous letter to the newspaper, pleading for a first-class high school for young women. The woman turned out to be Laura Cobb Rutherford, a member of two of the city's most prominent families. The letter moved her brother, the wealthy lawyer Thomas R. R. Cobb, to organize backers and raise funds to start such a school. In 1858, the Lucy Cobb Female Institute opened in a four-story building on eight acres of land west of Athens. The school was named for Cobb's daughter, Lucy, who died of scarlet fever at age thirteen while the school was being built. Guided by leaders such as Cobb's niece, Mildred Rutherford, who served the institute for forty-eight years as teacher, principal, president, and director, the Lucy Cobb Institute was one of the South's finest schools for girls, offering a rigorous academic curriculum that included science, math, languages, history, and literature. The school also emphasized the required social graces of the day, such as etiquette, manners, and proper decorum and attire. Institute alumnae became teachers, authors, businesswomen, and civic leaders, and one served in the U.S. House of Representatives.

Soon after becoming principal in 1880, Mildred Rutherford began raising money to build a chapel. She had her students write letters to prominent philanthropists around the country and seek donations, and an Athens girl named Nellie Stovall sent a request to George I. Seney of New York. Seney, who had previously donated to Emory University and Wesleyan College, promised $10,000 if the city of Athens would contribute $4,000. The local money was quickly raised, and work on the building, designed by William W. Thomas, an Athens engineer, began in 1882. With a capacity of 250, the chapel, which included a stage, was used for religious services for Lucy Cobb students and became a popular community venue for plays, pageants, lectures, and concerts.

Despite its great success, the Lucy Cobb Institute's fortunes declined in the early twentieth century. The death of Mildred Rutherford in 1928, along with financial difficulties brought on by the Depression and falling enrollment, forced its closure in 1931. Seney-Stovall Chapel remained open, but was used less and less, and by the end of World War II it had deteriorated to the point that it was shuttered. In the early 1950s, institute trustees turned the Lucy Cobb complex, including the chapel, over to UGA, which converted the buildings into offices, a dormitory, and a storage facility. By 1954, Lucy Cobb's top floor had become so unsafe that it had to be removed. Despite being listed on the National Register of Historic Places in 1972, both the institute and the chapel were in such disrepair by the late 1970s they were closed, and there was serious discussion of razing them. But in the early 1980s, dismayed citizens, led by the UGA history professor Phinizy Spalding (the grandson of Nellie Stovall), mounted an "I Love Lucy" campaign that raised $1 million from public and private donors to preserve the buildings. Congress appropriated an additional

My most vivid memory was when the end of
the Vietnam War was announced. Someone
who heard it on the radio told someone else,
and within a few hours everyone on campus
knew the war was over. The students that
were outside on campus grounds were danc-
ing and laughing and hugging each other.
Many students gathered together and went to
President Fred Davison's house and stood on
the lawn chanting, "The war is over, the war
is over!" Mr. Davison came to the door, and
everyone got really quiet. He asked, "What
do you students want?" One person said, "Sir,
if it is true that the Vietnam War is over, we
would like for you to cancel classes tomorrow
in celebration." President Davison said very
quietly, "I think that is an excellent idea. I will
cancel classes tomorrow." We all cheered and
thanked him as a group and went on our way.
It was a historic moment and a collective relief
to the student body that no more young men
and women would have to go to Vietnam to
fight a war.

B. T. Studdard, Class of 1976

$4.5 million in honor of the former Georgia congressman Carl Vinson, and in
1991 UGA's Institute of Government, named for Vinson, moved into the beau-
tifully restored institute building. The Vinson Institute is a major unit of the
university's public service and outreach program. The chapel was also fully
restored in 1997 and again hosts university and community events.

President's Home

BUILT: 1857–58 | LOCATION: 570 Prince Avenue | CURRENT USE: Residence of UGA presidents

Regarded as perhaps the finest example of Greek Revival architecture in
Athens, this magnificent mansion looks much as it did when the Athens railroad magnate John T. Grant built it for about $25,000 two years before the
Civil War. Set on five acres of land, the house is fronted by a meticulously
groomed formal boxwood garden, planted by Grant, who graduated from
UGA in 1833 and was married to the granddaughter of Georgia governor James
Jackson. The sweeping two-story portico, highlighted by towering Corinthian
columns, opens onto an entrance hall twelve feet wide and forty feet long with
fourteen-foot-high ceilings.

Elegantly furnished in a mid-Victorian style, the house, with some fifteen
thousand square feet of interior space, has porcelain china doorknobs, marble
fireplace mantels, door transoms with frosted glass, and heavily ornamented

cornices and ceiling medallions. Other features include an English Waterford crystal chandelier from 1810, a hand-blown Czechoslovakian lead crystal chandelier, and several French thumbprint chandeliers; a Louis XVI clock; a two-hundred-year-old set of china; a hand-painted Canton tray dating from the early Ming dynasty; and hand-painted French Zuber wallpaper depicting English hunting scenes. The rear yard includes two original outbuildings and manicured gardens with roses, camellias, azaleas, and other flowers. Grant sold the house and grounds in the 1860s to Benjamin H. Hill, a Georgia senator. They were later owned for many years by the family of the Athens banker James White. By World War II, the house had fallen into disrepair, and in 1949 the board of regents acquired it with a $35,000 gift from the W. C. Bradley Foundation of Columbus. The UGA Foundation provided another $50,000 to restore the house as a residence for UGA's president, and it is now listed on the National Register of Historic Places. The first presidential occupant was Jonathan C. Rogers, president from 1949 to 1950, and every president since has lived in the house.

UGA Health Sciences Campus

DATES FROM: 1860 | LOCATION: Normaltown section of Athens at the intersection of Prince and Oglethorpe Avenues | CURRENT USE: UGA/GRU Medical Partnership, UGA College of Public Health

On this historic fifty-six-acre complex, the University of Georgia / Georgia Regents University Medical Partnership is educating new physicians to help alleviate a severe shortage of doctors in Georgia, and UGA's College of Public Health is conducting research and providing training to address serious diseases and other medical issues in the state. These efforts will significantly alter the medical landscape in Georgia and help invigorate economic growth, lower health care costs, and improve quality of life for the state's citizens.

The conversion of this site into a health science center brings full circle UGA's involvement with this property. The university bought the land in 1860 to create a school known as the Collegiate Institute—a high school for boys who were not academically ready to enter the university. A building made with crushed stone and known as Rock College was erected in 1862, but was used mainly for military training during the Civil War. Federal troops kept a garrison on the property after the war. When the Collegiate Institute reopened, it served mainly Confederate veterans, but closed in 1872. The university then used the property as an experimental farm for several years. Later it was home

of the State Normal School, which trained young men and women to teach in rural areas, and the school's successor, the Georgia State Teachers College. By 1932, when a reorganization of state government created the University System of Georgia, the campus had grown to include ten major buildings, some made possible by private gifts, including $25,000 each from the United Daughters of the Confederacy and George Foster Peabody. With the formation of the University System of Georgia, the State Teachers College was absorbed into UGA's School of Education, and the state deeded the campus back to UGA. For the next twenty years the property was the UGA Coordinate Campus, where freshman and sophomore women lived.

In 1953, the property changed hands again when the university sold it to the federal government for $450,000 to be the site of a school to train U.S. Navy supply corps officers. The Navy School, as it was known, was an integral part of Athens for more than fifty years, employing about 130 military personnel and 190 civilians and hosting thousands of navy officers. But the school, falling victim to a federal military base realignment, in 2011 was moved to Newport, Rhode Island, allowing UGA to again acquire the property, this time for the Medical Partnership and College of Public Health.

Turning a military base into an academic campus for highly specialized medical instruction and research was a major challenge. Complicating the task was the fact that most of the buildings are old, some more than a century old.

A $20 million renovation begun in 2011 is converting the buildings for use as classrooms, lecture halls, laboratories, clinical and faculty offices, and other purposes. One building became a recreation and activity center for students; another was turned into a university day care center that accommodates 146 children. In keeping with pledges it made when assuming ownership of the property, the university has been diligent about preserving historic architectural and structural features of the buildings and maintaining the historic character and beauty of the campus. Units of the College of Public Health moved to the campus in early 2012, and the Medical Partnership followed later that year. Other units have moved as their facilities were readied. When the renovation work is completed in 2015, about fourteen hundred students, instructors, and staff members will occupy the campus.

State Botanical Garden of Georgia

BUILT: 1968 | LOCATION: 2450 South Milledge Avenue | CURRENT USE: Botanical research, recreation, tourist attraction

Acres of secluded forests, miles of quiet trails, abundant wildlife, rich collections of colorful flowers and rare and exotic plants, specialized research areas, striking architectural features, and scores of educational programs and activities: all these features and much more make the State Botanical Garden of Georgia the most heavily visited nonathletic attraction in Athens and one of UGA's crown jewels. Environmental education, plant conservation, habitat protection, and biodiversity are major themes of the garden, which the Georgia General Assembly designated in 1984 as the state's official botanical garden. Located about three miles southeast of the main campus, the garden spreads over 313 acres of mostly undisturbed woodlands, floodplains, hills, upland plateaus, marshes, and meadows.

Some five miles of trails, including about a mile along the bank of the Middle Oconee River, thread through forests of successional tree stages, ranging from century-old beeches to younger species growing in former cotton fields. Lurking in hiding places are rabbits, raccoons, opossums, beavers, foxes, and deer as well as snakes and other reptiles. Numerous bird species have earned the garden the Georgia Audubon Society's designation as an Important Bird Area. UGA faculty members and students use the garden as a living laboratory for teaching and research in plant biology and pathology, ecosystem studies, vegetation analysis, and environmental design. Scientists conduct

research on rare and endangered plant species of the Southeast and the conservation of native medicinal plant species. The garden has carefully cultivated growing areas for specialized collections of native flora, shade plants, heritage plants, herbs, and medicinal plants and flowers. The International Garden features plant species from around the world, and two special collections highlight rhododendrons and native azaleas.

The garden's centerpiece is the Alice Hand Callaway Visitor Center and Conservatory, a shimmering thirty-thousand-square-foot greenhouse harboring examples of dozens of tropical rain-forest species. The building has a gift shop, classrooms, a small theater, and a Great Room that is used for banquets, concerts, lectures, and other special events. Hidden deep in the garden's forest is the charming Day Chapel, built of cypress and other native woods and featuring magnificent carved mahogany and glass doors. The chapel's interior design motifs incorporate Georgia's state bird, tree, flower, and butterfly. Also on garden property is the headquarters building of the Garden Club of Georgia, featuring custom millwork, fine art, porcelains, and custom-designed carpets. Garden admission is free. For hours and more information, visit www .uga.edu/botgarden.

White Hall Mansion

BUILT: 1892 | NAMED FOR: John R. White, an Athens industrialist and business leader | LOCATION: Simonton Bridge Road and Whitehall Road | CURRENT USE: Private social and business events sponsored by the Warnell School of Forestry and Natural Resources

Disagreement once swirled over the unusual architectural style of this building, but John Waters, a UGA professor and historic preservation expert, has proclaimed it to be Victorian-Romanesque. Structures of this style have elements of ancient Roman architecture such as wide, rounded arches and stone masonry. White Hall is considered one of the finest examples of this architectural style in Georgia. The building's more than ten thousand square feet includes thirteen-foot-high rooms with ceiling beams, wainscoting, and stairways made of heavy white oak. The living room is finished in bird's-eye maple, the dining room in black cherry, and other trimmings in oak, walnut, and birch.

John R. White, born in 1847, built the house on land owned by his father. White was one of Athens's most prominent citizens in the last part of the nineteenth century, serving as a director of numerous businesses, including the National Bank of Athens and the Athens Railway and Electric Company,

which became part of the Georgia Power Company. The house remained in the White family until 1936, when it and 1,875 acres of nearby land were acquired by a state agency created to retire unusable farm land. The agency deeded the house and 750 acres to the University System of Georgia, which turned it over to UGA as an experimental forest. In 1976, the School of Forestry and Natural Resources used proceeds from the sale of insect-killed timber to restore the house, and in 1978 the school received an award from the Georgia Trust for Historic Preservation. The next year, White Hall was placed on the National Register of Historic Places. The building is not open to the public.

Chicopee Complex

BUILT: 1862 | NAMED FOR: Chicopee Mills, the former owner of the building |
LOCATION: East Broad Street and Martin Luther King Parkway | CURRENT USE: Facilities
Management Division, Office of Sustainability, Small Business Development Center, units of
the College of Agricultural and Environmental Sciences, Georgia Department of Economic
Development | BUILDING 0101

The brothers Ferdinand and Francis Cook, who operated a small armory in New Orleans that made weapons for the Confederate army, fled that city in 1862 just ahead of Union troops. They came to Athens and bought a small

Office of Sustainability

Cooperating closely with faculty members, students, administrators, and other departments, the Office of Sustainability is the standard bearer for environmental responsibility at UGA, working to implement principles and practices to help make the university one of America's greenest campuses.

Several campus groups, including an activist student group called the Go Green Alliance, began pushing for an office to coordinate and manage environmental issues and initiatives following a severe drought in 2007. After students voted in 2009 to pay a three-dollar-per-semester "green fee" to fund it, President Michael F. Adams established the Office of Sustainability in 2010 as part of the Facilities Management Division.

In addition to promoting practices such as water conservation, energy efficiency, recycling, and ecosystem protection, the office supports the university's teaching, research, and service missions. The office works with academic departments to integrate sustainability principles into more than sixty degree programs and ten interdisciplinary certificate programs with a sustainability focus. Faculty members and students receive assistance with research in such areas as water resources, bioenergy, climate change, and forest management, and the office supports more than twenty outreach programs that carry the university's resources and expertise in sustainability throughout the state to help citizens and communities.

The office sponsors or supports student environmental programs such as Earth Week, Recyclemania, Campus Sustainability Day, and Dawgs Ditch the Dumpster, and helped students start a successful recycling program for football home games. Staff members work closely with the University Architect's office and other Facilities Management departments to ensure that sustainability is incorporated into major construction, landscaping, transportation, and utility projects. These collaborative efforts have helped UGA make impressive advances in environmental stewardship:

- More than 1.5 million square feet of asphalt have been removed from the campus, and fifty acres of new green space have been added through sustainable redevelopment practices.
- Five major construction projects received gold certification—the highest level—under the LEED program. Two others earned lower certifications.
- Nearly half the garbage generated on campus is recycled, and a recycling goal of 65 percent has been set for 2020. Leaves, limbs, and other organic waste are composted at the Bioconversion Center, and plans are in place to compost food waste from dining halls.
- Water consumption has dropped nearly 30 percent through such conservation measures as the installation of fifty rain gardens and other storm-water management features, and fifteen cisterns that capture more than 530,000 gallons of rain and condensate for reuse.
- More than twenty miles of bike paths have been opened on campus. The university offers incentives to walk, bike, or bus to campus and promotes carpooling and ride sharing.

grist- and sawmill on the North Oconee River. They quickly enlarged it into this three-hundred-thousand-square-foot building, marked by a central stair tower and symmetrically arranged and proportioned doors and windows. Powered by the mill's waterwheels, the Cook and Brother Armory manufactured Enfield rifles, bayonets, and horseshoes for the Confederacy until 1864, when the business closed and many of its employees were organized into a Confederate army unit. In 1870, the Athens Manufacturing Company, the city's oldest business, bought the building and turned it into a mill that spun and wove cotton and wool textiles and rope. Known as the Athens Factory (and as the Check Factory for the design of its popular gingham cloth), the mill converted from waterpower to coal power and operated through the Depression. In 1947, the building was sold to Chicopee Mills, a division of Johnson and Johnson, and from 1950 to 1979 workers manufactured bandage gauze and material used as backing for wallpaper and box springs. Chicopee donated the building—and the associated warehouses and other structures, which occupied 26.6 acres—to UGA in 1980. At the time it was believed to be the largest single gift from a private concern to a school in the University System of Georgia. UGA extensively renovated the building in an attempt to preserve its historic character and restore architectural features. Considered an outstanding example of adaptive use, Chicopee recalls both the vital role of manufacturing in Athens's early years and an era when water was a primary power source.

When the Office of Sustainability, which manages university environmental initiatives, moved into Chicopee in 2010, employees decided to use recycled scrap and surplus materials to construct their workspace. Discarded wooden doors were turned into desktops, and old wooden handrails became part of a conference room wall. Carpet remnants from other construction projects cover the floor. Desk dividers made from renewable cork tiles are in holders made of recycled steel.

The Facilities Management Division, known before 2012 as the Physical Plant, maintains and manages the university's physical facilities, including buildings, grounds, and utilities. The division's responsibilities include building maintenance, repair, and alterations; campus mechanical and electrical systems; the central steam and chiller plants, which heat and cool buildings; custodial services; engineering support; the maintenance of grounds, landscaping, and streets; and the operation of an automotive maintenance shop, a vehicle rental fleet, and a construction materials warehouse.

The Iron Horse

In a cornfield off Georgia Highway 15 in Greene County, about fifteen miles south of Athens, stands a modernistic metal sculpture of a horse that many consider the legacy of one of UGA's more ignominious moments. The Iron Horse, as the statue is known, weighs more than a ton, stands eleven feet tall, and is twelve feet long. It was created in 1954 by the Chicago sculptor Abbott Pattison, who was a visiting professor in the UGA Art Department. A respected artist whose works are in Tokyo, China, Buckingham Palace, and U.S. museums, Pattison welded together pieces of black steel into the abstract form of a horse. Abstraction was considered avant-garde by some in Athens at the time, and some UGA students weren't ready for modern art. Pattison had ruffled feathers by publicly criticizing students' lack of cultural sophistication, and when his sculpture was put on display in the Reed Hall quadrangle, students retaliated. They stuffed hay in the horse's mouth, beat it with clubs, and showered it with paint. Then they tried to burn it by using automobile tires as fuel. Firemen had to disperse the crowd with hoses.

The incident, reported by the press in Georgia and even by *Time* magazine, prompted the university to hide the sculpture in an off-campus location for five years. In 1959, a UGA horticulture professor, L. C. Curtis, asked whether he could take the horse to his Greene County farm so that passing motorists on the nearby highway could see it. The university agreed, and in the dark of night the Iron Horse was trucked out of Athens. But its troubles weren't over. After it was placed in the field, vandals repeatedly came in the night and pushed it over, finally forcing Curtis to set the sculpture in concrete embedded in an underground trench. There have been several attempts to return the horse to campus, but the Curtis family has refused to let it go. In 2012, UGA bought the six-hundred-acre Curtis farm to use for crop research. But the sale allowed the family to retain ownership of the Iron Horse and the four hundred square feet around it, ensuring that the statue will remain a popular landmark. The family has always insisted that nothing should be read into the fact that the horse's backside is toward Athens—that is just how it came off the truck.

CHAPTER 7   Athletic Facilities

A BRIGHT SUN warms the chill off a crisp October afternoon. In Sanford Stadium, ninety-three thousand people—most dressed in red—enjoy the Redcoat Band's spirited pregame show. A hush falls over the crowd as a lone trumpeter in the southwest corner of the upper deck sends the soulful opening notes of "The Battle Hymn of the Bulldog Nation" wafting over the stadium. Fans erupt in an ear-splitting roar as Larry Munson recalls the heroics of gridiron stars whose feats flash across the giant end-zone screen. A few moments later, all those whose blood runs red and black are on their feet and making Sanford Stadium noise as the Redcoats strike up "Glory, Glory" and the Georgia Bulldogs burst onto the field behind Hairy Dawg and somersaulting cheerleaders.

There are many who say that if they don't live a good enough life to get into heaven, Sanford Stadium on an October Saturday afternoon is their second choice.

Athletics have long been an integral part of life at UGA. When the university reopened after the Civil War, students formed baseball clubs that traveled to other cities to compete. The entire student body and many Athens citizens turned out for the annual Field Day, which featured track and field events, a greased-pig chase, and a picnic. Baseball became the university's first intercollegiate sport in 1886 when a team coached by "Hustlin" Hughie Jennings posted a 2–0 record; football came next, and other teams soon followed: track and field (1897); tennis (1898); basketball (1905); golf (1924); and swimming and diving (1926). The Georgia Athletic Association was formed in 1929 to provide management and funding for the growing athletic program.

All the early teams were solely male. Women were admitted as regular university students in 1918, but were permitted to compete in sports only among themselves on intramural and club teams operated by the Physical Education Department. Women's intercollegiate competition did not begin until 1967, when Liz Murphey was hired to coach the women's club golf team, which joined the Association for Intercollegiate Athletics for Women (AIAW).

Later, women's club teams in tennis, swimming and diving, volleyball, and basketball also joined the AIAW. Murphey was a leader in the university's implementation of Title IX, the 1972 law that requires nondiscrimination in funding, equipment, and facilities for men's and women's athletic programs. She became the coordinator of club sports and then assistant athletic director for women's sports when the Athletic Association absorbed club sports in 1978. In 1982, the association moved women's teams from the AIAW to the National Collegiate Athletic Association (NCAA). As women's athletics grew in popularity and success, more teams were added: gymnastics (1984), soccer (1994), softball (1996), and equestrian (2001).

The 1894 football team

Though the university was racially integrated in 1961, it was not until 1968 that Harry Sims, a young African American from Athens, walked on for the track team to become the first black student-athlete. The following year, Maxie Foster, also from Athens, received a grant in aid to compete in track, becoming the first black student-athlete to receive an athletic scholarship. Ronnie Hogue, who played on the basketball team in 1970, was the first African American to compete in a major sport. In 1971, the first black football players received scholarships.

Today, with more than six hundred student-athletes, some of the best collegiate sports venues in the country, and some of the most respected and successful coaches in the college ranks, UGA boasts one of the nation's outstanding athletic programs. Georgia's twenty-one varsity teams have won thirty-nine national championships and dozens of Southeastern Conference titles. Nine teams have won one or more national titles, and fifteen have captured one or more SEC crowns.

UGA student-athletes have received more NCAA and National Football Foundation postgraduate scholarships, NCAA Top Eight Awards, and Academic All-America honors than any school in the South. Scores of student-athletes have been named to all-America and Academic All-America teams, and many have gone on to successful professional athletic careers and been inducted into collegiate and professional halls of fame. Widely respected for its integrity, sound business operation, and commitment to academic achievement and overall excellence, UGA's athletic program ranks among the nation's best.

Varsity athletic facilities are located on the Central, South, and East Campuses and at several off-campus locations. This chapter describes those facilities and includes information on the history and success of UGA's athletic teams.

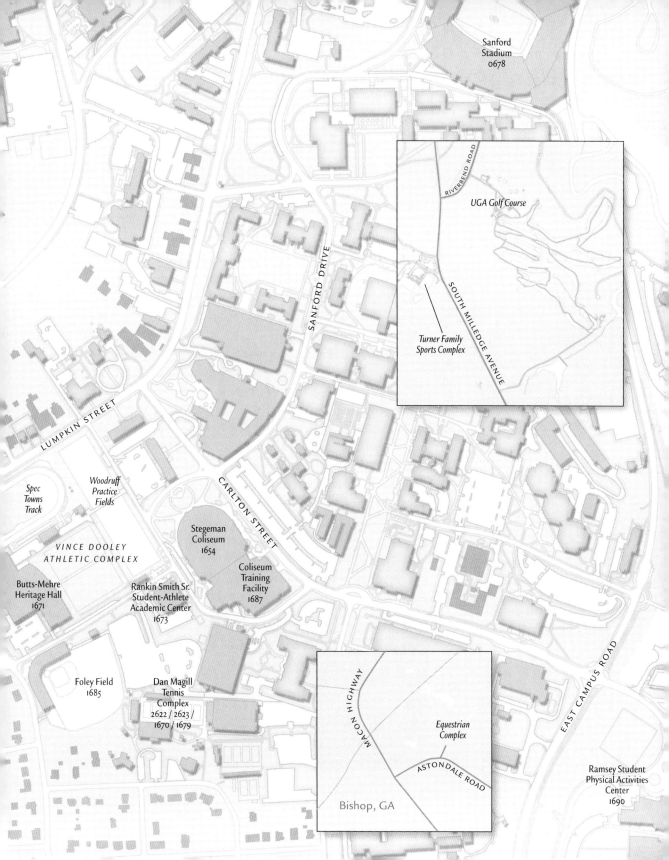

Sanford
Stadium
0678

RIVERBEND ROAD

UGA Golf Course

SANFORD DRIVE

*Turner Family
Sports Complex*

SOUTH MILLEDGE AVENUE

LUMPKIN STREET

*Spec
Towns
Track*

*Woodruff
Practice
Fields*

CARLTON STREET

*VINCE DOOLEY
ATHLETIC COMPLEX*

Stegeman
Coliseum
1654

Butts-Mehre
Heritage Hall
1671

Rankin Smith Sr.
Student-Athlete
Academic Center
1673

Coliseum
Training
Facility
1687

Foley Field
1685

Dan Magill
Tennis
Complex
2622 / 2623 /
1670 / 1679

MACON HIGHWAY

*Equestrian
Complex*

ASTONDALE ROAD

Bishop, GA

EAST CAMPUS ROAD

Ramsey Student
Physical Activities
Center
1690

Olympic Gold Medal Soccer Game

The 76,481 fans who watched the women's soccer final of the Atlanta Olympics in Sanford Stadium on August 1, 1996, was at the time the largest number of people ever to attend a women's sports event. An estimated three billion people around the world watched the game on television.

UGA *Memory*

My favorite memory at UGA occurred during every home football game. There was nothing better than waking up on Saturday morning and listening to the pregame Bulldawg show on the radio and hearing all the great Bulldawg songs to get me fired up. These songs would carry me through the morning as I got ready for my date to pick me up and begin the tradition of a pregame meal at a fraternity house and then walk down to the stadium. I also loved hearing Queen's "We are the Champions" played at every game because we went 12–0 in that glorious 1980 season!

Jodi Selvey, Class of 1984

Sanford Stadium

BUILT: 1929 | LOCATION: Central Campus | NAMED FOR: Steadman V. Sanford, UGA president, 1932–35 | CURRENT USE: Home of Bulldog football team | BUILDING 0678

Excitement, pride, tradition, and superb athleticism come together on Saturdays in the fall in what is often cited as one of the most beautiful collegiate stadiums in the country. Sanford Stadium was constructed at a cost of $360,000 to replace a smaller stadium nearby known as Sanford Field. Clarke County government workers and convict laborers (a common practice at the time) used axes, shovels, and mule-drawn wagons to excavate the natural valley between North and South Campuses and reroute Tanyard Branch, which flowed through the ravine. Built to hold thirty thousand spectators, the stadium hosted its first game on October 12, 1929, when the all-American end Vernon "Catfish" Smith scored all of Georgia's points in a 15–0 victory over Yale. Since then, the Bulldogs have won more than three hundred home games.

Field-level lights installed in 1940 enabled night games to be played, and the stadium was double-decked in 1967, adding nineteen thousand seats. In 1981, the east end zone was enclosed, adding another nineteen thousand seats but disbanding the raucous "track people" who for years watched games for free from the railroad embankment east of the stadium. With sky suites and other additions, Sanford Stadium now holds nearly ninety-three thousand, making it one of the ten largest collegiate stadiums in the country and the third largest in the Southeastern Conference. Average attendance for Georgia home games consistently ranks in the top ten in the country.

Steadman Sanford, a member of a family associated with UGA since the early nineteenth century, was born in 1871 and joined the faculty in 1903. He

Militia at Sanford Field, ca. 1913

"Between the Hedges"

The famous hedges encircling the Sanford Stadium field were only a foot high when they were planted for the stadium's first game in 1929. Charlie E. Martin, the athletic business manager at the time, got the idea after seeing the hedge of roses at the Rose Bowl in Pasadena, California. Since roses aren't suited to Georgia's climate, horticulturists suggested a plant more common in the state—a type of privet known as Chinese ligustrum. A small wooden fence protected the plants when they were first installed. Today, a wire fence is concealed within the five thousand square feet of hedges around the field. Only three specially selected groundskeepers are permitted to prune the hedges to maintain their uniform square shape. Only once have the iconic hedges been removed—to widen the field for Olympic soccer competition in the summer of 1996. Cuttings from original hedges were taken to then-secret nurseries in Thomson, Georgia, and Quincy, Florida, where they grew into a new generation of plants used to create "Hedges II," which was installed shortly before the first home game in 1996. The phrase "between the hedges" is said to have originated in the early 1930s when a newspaper sportswriter, referring to an upcoming home game, wrote that "the Bulldogs will have their opponent between the hedges."

was the founder and first dean of the School of Journalism and served as dean of the university before becoming president. A strong proponent of college athletics, he served as faculty chairman of athletics and was the major force behind the construction of Sanford Stadium, which he vowed would be the "best football stadium in Dixie." He helped start the Southeastern Conference and was president of the NCAA. Sanford stepped down as university president in 1935 to become chancellor of the University System of Georgia, a position he held until his death, ten years later.

UGA's storied football program is rich in tradition and success. The Bulldogs have won more than 730 games, giving them one of the highest winning percentages and best total victory records in college football. The Bulldogs have won twelve SEC championships and played in forty-eight bowl games (ranking sixth nationally), and Coach Vince Dooley's 1980 team was the consensus national champion. Reflecting the program's commitment to academic success, Georgia leads the nation in the number of football players receiving NCAA Post-Graduate Scholarships (thirteen) and National Football Foundation Post-Graduate Scholarships (eleven). UGA ranks fourth in the number of football Academic All-Americans (eighteen), and scores of Bulldog players have earned Academic All-SEC honors. Two Georgia football players— Frank Sinkwich and Herschel Walker—won college football's highest honor, the Heisman Trophy, and Walker and Charley Trippi received the Maxwell Trophy as national player of the year. Sixty-eight Bulldogs have been named to all-America teams, several hundred have been chosen all-SEC, and sixteen players and coaches are in the College Football Hall of Fame.

My favorite moment was when UGA finally beat Tennessee in football in the year 2000 after a nine-year losing streak. I remember going to prior games and getting beat up on by legends Peyton Manning and Tee Martin. What made some of those games even worse is when the UT fans would hold up a number at the end of the game showing what the streak was at (6, 7, 8 . . .) as we were walking out of the stadium. As a competitive guy, it was embarrassing and I felt awful. Then the year 2000. As in most close games, we were cautiously optimistic, but also thinking UT would pull out the win, as good teams usually do. Well, as the final horn sounded, UGA had finally won, 21–10! Now, I wouldn't consider myself a person who follows the crowd, but as I was in the end zone near the bridge and the kids all around me started rushing the field, I thought, "Why not?" I got down to the railing and saw the huge hedges in front of me and did a double take, thinking I couldn't make the jump. But then I just went for it and cleared with inches to spare. On the field there were people just running around hugging and high-fiving people. Some decided to start climbing the goalposts, but I wasn't about to start damaging Sanford Stadium. All in all, it was something I'll remember for quite a while, not to mention being the first and last time that the goalposts were taken down because of fans rushing the field (unlike Tech fans, who do it once a year). So that was a great memory of my time at UGA, where everyone was together and celebrating after a decade of misery.

Jim Gassman, Class of 2002

Vince Dooley Athletic Complex

DEDICATED: 2008 | NAMED FOR: Vince Dooley, former football coach and athletic director | LOCATION: South Campus

The Vince Dooley Athletic Complex honors one of the most accomplished, influential, and popular figures in the history of UGA athletics. As head football coach from 1964 to 1988, and athletic director from 1979 to 2004, Dooley was instrumental in turning UGA into a national pacesetter in collegiate athletic excellence. His coaching record of 201-77-10—the best in Georgia history—includes the 1980 national championship, six SEC championships, and twenty bowl appearances. He coached forty first-team all-Americans, including the Heisman Trophy and Maxwell Award winner Herschel Walker, and ten Academic All-Americans. He was National Coach of the Year in 1980 and SEC Coach of the Year seven times.

During Dooley's tenure as athletic director, UGA won twenty-three national championships, including an unprecedented four in the 1998–99 academic year, and seventy-eight SEC team titles, along with numerous individual national and conference titles in both men's and women's sports. Dooley's staunch commitment to academic success for student-athletes resulted in more than one hundred student-athletes being named first-team Academic All-Americans and more than fifty receiving NCAA Post-Graduate Scholarships. Expenditures on construction, additions, and improvements to athletic facilities totaled nearly $80 million under Dooley, and the Athletic Association contributed more than $2 million for nonathletic scholarships and the construction of nonathletic facilities. Dooley established an endowment fund for the university libraries with a personal gift of $100,000 and helped the fund grow to more than $4 million.

A member of the College Football Hall of Fame, the Marine Corps Sports Hall of Fame, and both the Georgia and Alabama sports halls of fame, Dooley is the only person to be president of both the American Football Coaches Association and the National Association of Collegiate Directors of Athletics. As president of the coaches association and chair of NCAA football committees on rules and recruitment, he pushed for higher national academic standards for student athletes and also for reforms in recruiting practices. Among his many honors are the highest accolades of his profession, including the Amos Alonzo Stagg Award from the American Football Coaches Association, for lifetime contributions to the sport of football; the Bear Bryant Lifetime Achievement Award, for excellence in coaching on and off the field; and the

Uga, Georgia's Famous Mascot

In the 1997 movie *Midnight in the Garden of Good and Evil*, one of the film's characters, a Savannah antiques dealer, tells a visiting New York writer, John Kelso, "No matter what you and I ever do in our lives, Mr. Kelso, neither of us will ever be as famous as Uga, the university mascot of the Georgia Bulldogs."

Uga is indeed one of the best-known collegiate mascots in the country. But with his spiked collar, red sweater, and friendly personality, he is more than just a mascot. He is a cuddly, pug-faced, one-dog ambassador for the spirit, tradition, history, and pride that are hallmarks of the University of Georgia.

The subject of books, countless newspaper and magazine articles, and many television appearances, Uga has visited the Georgia General Assembly (with Vince Dooley after the 1980 football national championship), the Heisman Trophy banquet (with Herschel Walker in 1982), the NCAA basketball Final Four tournament (with Georgia's only Final Four team in 1983), and the Senate Office Building in Washington, D.C. (with Georgia congressmen). A photograph of him lunging at an Auburn football player in 1996 made him a national sensation. The next year, *Sports Illustrated* declared him the nation's best college mascot and put him on its cover. He even made a cameo appearance in *Midnight in the Garden of Good and Evil*.

Though it is hard to imagine the University of Georgia without Uga, a bulldog hasn't always been the mascot. Reportedly, the mascot for Georgia's first intercollegiate football game was a goat. The origin of having a bulldog as the mascot is often traced to an article in the *Atlanta Journal*, dated November 3, 1920, that suggested that "the Georgia Bulldogs would sound good because there is a certain dignity about a bulldog, as well as ferocity."

Bulldog mascot Uga IX

But there wasn't an official bulldog mascot until years later. Fans sometimes brought their dogs to games to serve as a mascot. A brindled English bulldog named Mike lived in the football field house and was cared for by players until he died in 1955. He is depicted in the bronze statue on the north side of Memorial Hall.

The modern line of Ugas began in 1956 when Frank Seiler of Savannah, then a UGA law student, and his wife, Cecelia, offered their pet bulldog as the mascot. That dog, born December 2, 1955, was registered as Hood's Ole Dan, but was given the mascot name Uga I. A succession of direct descendants followed, each with a kennel name but also identified by Uga and a Roman numeral (Uga II, Uga III, etc.). Ugas are family pets and live with the Seilers in Savannah when they are not working as the mascot.

When Ugas die, they are entombed in marble vaults embedded in the wall on the southwest end of Sanford Stadium near the Main Gate. Laid to rest in a solemn burial ceremony, each dog receives an engraved epitaph on its vault, and fans often decorate the vaults with flowers on game days. The University of Georgia is the only major university that buries its mascots in the confines of its football stadium.

I was a student at UGA between 1968 and
1972. There was one home football game
when we were playing Ole Miss. It was halftime, and as was the tradition, fans and
special guests walked around the outside
of the hedges. As Uga was escorted around,
all stood up, with yells of "Damn Good
Dog" bouncing off the stadium walls. I sat
back down and leaned over to mix another
drink when the audience went nuts. A loud
crescendo of "Damn Good Chicken" was
deafening. I had no idea what was going on.
I stood up, and there walking around the
hedges was Colonel Sanders, all decked out
in his traditional white suit with his trade-
mark goatee, waving to the crowds with his
cane. What a great moment!

Henry (Hank) Mitchell, Class of 1972

John L. Toner Award, presented by the National Football Foundation and
College Football Hall of Fame.

The entrance to the Dooley Athletic Complex at the intersection of
Lumpkin Street and Pinecrest Drive is marked by a bronze sculpture depicting Dooley atop the shoulders of players Tim Morris and Jeff Harper following the national championship victory at the Sugar Bowl in New Orleans on
January 1, 1981. Created by the Athens sculptor Stan Mullins, the statue is surrounded by a landscaped garden reflecting Dooley's passion for horticulture
and gardening.

The Dooley Athletic Complex includes Butts-Mehre Heritage Hall, Spec
Towns Track, the Woodruff Practice Fields, Stegeman Coliseum, the Coliseum
Training Facility, the Rankin Smith Student-Athlete Academic Center, Foley
Baseball Field, and the Dan Magill Tennis Complex.

Butts-Mehre Heritage Hall

BUILT: 1987, with a major addition completed in 2012 | NAMED FOR: Football coaches
Wallace Butts and Harry Mehre | CURRENT USE: UGA football program, Bulldog athletic
museum | BUILDING 1671

Butts-Mehre is the shrine of Georgia athletics, a striking black marble edifice
that symbolizes the tradition, strength, and excellence of one of the nation's
premier collegiate athletic programs. The original seventy-eight-thousand-
square-foot building, enlarged with a $40 million, fifty-three-thousand-
square-foot addition, is home base for the football team. It boasts a weight
room, coaches' offices, and a sports medicine area with dedicated spaces for
treatment, rehabilitation, hydrotherapy, and taping. The locker room features a lounge, televisions, computer stations, and video game stations. The
team meeting room, which is equipped for showing game films and motiva-
tional videos, is used also for press conferences. A large multipurpose room
with a thirty-yard synthetic-turf floor allows for indoor practices. The Larry
Munson Trophy Room, named for the beloved late "Voice of the Bulldogs,"
displays scores of football awards and prizes, including the 1980 National
Championship Trophy.

Beneath a domed roof on the ground floor is the Georgia Bulldog Hall
of Fame, whose exhibits and memorabilia highlight great moments and
legendary figures for all Georgia athletic teams. The building also contains
administrative offices of the Georgia Athletic Association.

Butts-Mehre is named for two of Georgia's most famous football coaches. Wallace (Wally) Butts compiled a 140–86–9 record while coaching from 1939 to 1960. His teams won four SEC championships and played in eight bowls, and his 1942 team was declared national champion in six polls. After stepping down as coach, Butts was athletic director for three years. Harry Mehre coached from 1928 to 1937 and had a record of 59–34–6, including a victory over Yale in the first game in Sanford Stadium. Mehre's five straight wins over Yale, and victories over other major schools, helped put Georgia in the national spotlight as a rising football power.

Spec Towns Track

BUILT: 1964 | NAMED FOR: Forrest "Spec" Towns, UGA track star and coach | CURRENT USE: UGA track and field teams

Track and field is UGA's third-oldest varsity sport. The program grew out of intramural field days held in the late 1800s that featured events such as wrestling, tug-of-war, and a greased-pig chase. A UGA team competed in its first

intercollegiate track contest in 1897. The following year, UGA defeated Georgia Tech in the teams' first dual meet and went on to enjoy an undefeated season. Early teams practiced and competed on Herty Field on North Campus, moving in 1911 to Sanford Field, and later to a track constructed nearby. After World War II, the team inherited a track that the U.S. Navy had built for its preflight training school, located where the bookstore and the Tate Student Center now stand. In 1965, the team moved to the current location, which was named for Towns in 1990. Upgraded with a $3 million renovation after the 2009 season, the facility has a state-of-the-art four-hundred-meter track with eight running lanes. Other features include two throwing circles with cages; five vaulting areas; four long jump areas; two high jump pits; two javelin runways; a shot put area; and a one-thousand-seat grandstand.

The men's and women's track and field teams have each won an SEC outdoor championship and have finished in the top ten in NCAA national championship meets. Together the teams have captured thirty-six NCAA individual or team titles in indoor or outdoor competition. Altogether, 298 male and female track and field athletes have won all-America honors.

Spec Towns, a native of Fitzgerald, Georgia, won two national championships in the high hurdles at UGA and led the 1937 team to its first SEC title. He won the gold medal in the 120-yard hurdles at the 1936 Berlin Olympic Games (attended by Adolph Hitler) and later set a world record in the 110-meter high hurdles while winning more than sixty consecutive races. While coaching from 1938 to 1975, the longest tenure of any UGA track coach, his athletes won twenty-nine individual SEC titles. Towns is in the USA Track and Field Hall of Fame and the Georgia Sports Hall of Fame.

Georgia's cross-country program, which trains off campus, has made marked advances in recent years and is one of the country's most competitive. Five Bulldog runners have been all-America selections, more than thirty have been chosen all-SEC, and many have been named NCAA all-region performers. Georgia women runners were chosen as SEC freshmen of the year for three consecutive years, 2002–4, and Sarah Madebach was the SEC female cross-country athlete of the year in 2007.

Woodruff Practice Fields

BUILT: early 1940s | NAMED FOR: George "Kid" Woodruff, a UGA football player and coach | CURRENT USE: Practice fields for the football team

The Woodruff fields were built for use by cadets in the navy preflight training school, and the football team inherited them after World War II. One of the three full-length fields is natural grass; the other two are covered with artificial turf. The natural field is irrigated by water collected in a two-hundred-thousand-gallon underground cistern installed as part of the expansion of Butts-Mehre Heritage Hall. Woodruff, the captain of the 1911 football team, was a business executive in Columbus, Georgia, who coached as a hobby and was paid one dollar a year as coach from 1923 to 1927. He compiled a 32-16-1 record, and his 1927 team went 9-1, won the Southern Conference championship, and was named national champion in two polls. Woodruff later served for thirty years as chair of the Georgia Student Educational Fund, which raised money for student athletic scholarships.

Redcoat Marching Band

"Keep your seats, everyone—the Redcoats are coming!"

With that famous introduction, the four-hundred-member UGA Redcoat Band steps smartly onto the Sanford Stadium field for a pregame or halftime show marked by precision marching, intricate formations, and rousing music. From the peppy chords of "Glory, Glory" to the melancholy strains of "Tara's Theme," the Redcoats strike the musical spark that ignites Bulldog spirit and energy on Saturday afternoons in the fall. The band, which celebrated its centennial in 2005, has played in most major football bowl games, marched in President Jimmy Carter's inaugural parade, and in 2006 became the first U.S. college band to give a marching-band performance in China. In 2000, the Redcoats were the first Southeastern Conference band to win the Sudler Trophy, the top national honor for a college marching band. Only about a third of band members are music majors, but despite six to eight hours of rehearsal each week, many maintain some of the highest academic averages at the university.

Today's crisp, colorful Redcoats are far removed from the twenty young men who formed a ragtag marching ensemble for university military cadets in 1905. That group's first nonmilitary performance, at a Georgia-Clemson baseball game in 1906, resulted in its mandatory appearance at athletic events for the next twenty-five years. The band remained part of the military department until the mid-1930s, when alumni and the Athletic Association began providing support for uniforms and instruments and the ensemble adopted the name Georgia Marching Band. A newspaper reporter's reference to the "red-coated band," and the group's frequent playing of the song "Dixie," led to the band being known as the Dixie Redcoats until "Dixie" was dropped in the 1970s as being racially objectionable. Under Roger Dancz, who led the band from 1955 to 1991, the Redcoats were known for spectacular halftime shows, including a 1978 show featuring an actual marriage ceremony on the field. Dancz's wife, Phyllis, was instrumental in creating the band's popular auxiliary units, the Georgettes, Majorettes, Flagline, and Feature Twirlers. Small groups of Redcoats perform as pep bands at basketball games, volleyball matches, and other university and community events. Several hundred former band members belong to the Redcoat Alumni Association, which fields an alumni band for the homecoming game each year.

Stegeman Coliseum

BUILT: 1964 | NAMED FOR: Herman J. Stegeman, football coach and dean of men | CURRENT USE: Men's and women's basketball, women's gymnastics, commencement, and major campus and community events | BUILDING 1654

Considered one of the best indoor sports arenas in the South when it opened, Stegeman Coliseum is now one of the region's oldest venues for college basketball. But age doesn't dampen the ardor of fans, or the grit and skill of athletes, as the venerable building springs to raucous life for Bulldog basketball games and gymnastics meets.

With its sweeping, undulating roof anchored by massive concrete columns, the building was an architectural oddity when it opened. But the design concealed an innovative engineering feat: the coliseum is actually two separate structures. The circular roof, four hundred feet in diameter, and the building below it are connected only by an aluminum bellows that seals the joints and allows the roof to rise and fall with temperature changes. The first basketball game played in the coliseum, on February 22, 1964, drew 13,200 people—at the time the largest crowd ever to watch an indoor sporting event in Georgia—to cheer the Bulldogs to an 81–68 victory over Georgia Tech. Since then, such hoops legends as Shaquille O'Neal, Pete Maravich, Dominique Wilkins, Teresa

Olympics Monument

The most prominent legacy of the competitions that UGA hosted for the 1996 Centennial Olympics is the large black marble monument on the Stegeman Coliseum's west lawn, which was designed by the UGA art professor Jack Kehoe. Inscribed on one side of the wall, in eleven languages, are words or characters for five universal passions: awe, anguish, love, triumph, and joy. On the other side are the names of more than 115 UGA students who have competed in the modern Olympics, beginning with the track star Forrest "Spec" Towns in 1936.

My name is John Carter. I graduated in 1994
with a degree in political science and a minor
in Mandarin. One of my favorite memories is
of going onto the roof of the coliseum. The
bars on the back columns used to be bent out
enough to squeeze through. Friends and I
would go up there at night. While not entirely
legal, it was certainly quiet, peaceful, and a
great way to end an evening.

John Carter, Class of 1994

Edwards, and Katrina McClain have dribbled and dunked in the coliseum, and some of the nation's best female collegiate gymnasts have vaulted and tumbled their way to national championships. The building has hosted numerous NCAA tournament basketball games for men and women as well as conference, regional, and national gymnastics championship tournaments.

More than just athletes have rocked the coliseum. For years it was the major campus venue for concerts, hosting such stars as Louis Armstrong, Johnny Mathis, Ray Charles, Bob Hope, Kenny Rogers, the Allman Brothers, and Outkast. An annual rodeo and livestock show sponsored by the agriculture college were held in the building for many years, and in 1999 a standing-room-only crowd jammed the building for a speech by former Soviet premier Mikhail Gorbachev. University and local high school commencement exercises, along with large community events, are held in the building, which has undergone many changes and upgrades, including extensive improvements before hosting women's volleyball and rhythmic gymnastics in the 1996 Olympics. A $3.6 million renovation to the building in 2010 raised its seating capacity to 10,523.

Herman Stegeman came to UGA in 1919 to establish a physical training program for ROTC cadets. He stayed to coach Georgia's football team from 1920 to 1922, compiling a 20–6–3 record and winning the Southern Conference Championship. He was also head coach for baseball and track, and his .686 winning percentage as basketball coach is one of the best in program history. He coached the 1937 track team to the SEC men's championship. After coaching, Stegeman served as athletic director and later as dean of male students. He was the namesake of Stegeman Hall, a building constructed on Central Campus during World War II; it was the home of the university's athletic and physical education departments until its demolition in 1995. On March 2, 1996, the coliseum was named for Stegeman.

Basketball began at UGA in 1905 when a men's team began playing in the Athens YMCA. From 1911 to 1919, games were played in the building that is now Memorial Hall, and later in a gym on the third floor of a building in downtown Athens. The team's first permanent home was Woodruff Hall, a barnlike wooden gymnasium that opened in 1925 in the Central Campus area where the Psychology-Journalism Building stands. Woodruff was demolished after the coliseum opened in 1964. The Bulldog men's basketball team has won two SEC tournament championships and played in eleven NCAA tournaments, reaching the Final Four in 1983. Seven men's players have been named all-Americans, and eighty-four have received all-SEC honors. Several former Bulldogs have played professional basketball.

Women's basketball was limited mainly to competition with in-state schools until 1979, when Andy Landers became the first full-time head coach. Under Landers, the Lady Dogs soon became a perennial national power, winning the National Women's Invitational Tournament in his second year and reaching the championship game in the 1985 NCAA national tournament. Landers's teams have appeared in twenty-eight NCAA tournaments altogether (making the Final Four five times) and have won eleven SEC championship and tournament titles, the second-highest total of any conference school. With more than 820 victories at UGA and an average of 24.2 wins per season (third best among all Division I coaches with as long a tenure), Landers has been named national coach of the year four times. Among the many all-Americans he has coached are two all-time greats in women's collegiate basketball: Teresa Edwards, who won four gold and one bronze Olympic medals and is the only U.S. basketball player—male or female—to compete in five Olympic Games; and Katrina McClain, who won Olympic gold medals in 1988 and 1996 and a bronze in 1992.

Coliseum Training Facility

BUILT: 2007 | CURRENT USE: Practice facility for men's and women's basketball and women's gymnastics | BUILDING 1687

This $30 million, 120,000-square-foot facility provides the basketball and gymnastics teams with superb practice space and support services. The men's and women's basketball teams have their own gyms, with full-length courts and four side goals. Between the gyms is a state-of-the-art audio-video area and training room, and nearby are locker rooms, lounges, staff offices, and space for team meetings. The first floor has a large weight room and short sprint track. Great moments and achievements in Bulldog basketball history are featured in colorful displays, memorabilia, photos, and interactive video kiosks.

A prominent part of the training facility is the Suzanne Yoculan Gymnastics Center, which includes a sixteen-thousand-square-foot gym, locker rooms, offices, study areas, a team lounge, and a theater-style meeting room. The gym has self-contained training areas for each apparatus on which gymnasts compete.

Yoculan led the Gym Dogs from 1983 to 2009, becoming one of the most successful coaches in NCAA gymnastics history. Her teams won ten national championships, including five consecutive titles (2005–9), twenty-one NCAA regional championships, and sixteen SEC titles. She had four undefeated

seasons, and her teams finished in the top three nationally nineteen of her final twenty-one years. She was national gymnastics coach of the year five times and SEC coach of the year eight times. Bulldog gymnasts lead the nation with thirty-eight individual NCAA titles. Sixty-one gymnasts have earned 313 all-America honors, forty-eight have been chosen National Scholar Athletes, and five have received a prestigious NCAA Post-Graduate Scholarship.

Rankin Smith Sr. Student-Athlete Academic Center

BUILT: 2002 | NAMED FOR: Rankin M. Smith Sr., an Atlanta businessman | CURRENT USE: Tutoring and academic assistance for student-athletes | BUILDING 1673

This building sits on the site previously occupied by a field house constructed for the navy preflight training school. After World War II, the football team used the building as a field house, and in 1969 it became the Alumni House, home of the university's alumni office. The building was razed in 2000 and replaced by this facility, which was partly funded by a $3.5 million gift from members of the Rankin M. Smith Sr. family. The center serves more than six hundred student-athletes whose scholarships and varsity athletic programs are administered through the Georgia Athletic Association. Students attend individual and group tutoring sessions and study in a computer lab and a "smart classroom" equipped with audiovisual technology. Other features include a writing center, offices for counselors, and a 250-seat assembly hall.

Rankin Smith Sr., who was president and CEO of Life Insurance Company of Georgia, attended UGA and was an ardent fan and supporter of the athletic program. A trustee of the UGA Foundation and the Georgia Student Educational Fund, he was owner and chair of the Atlanta Falcons football team from 1965 until his death in 1997.

Foley Field

BUILT: 1966 | NAMED FOR: Frank D. Foley, UGA baseball player | CURRENT USE: UGA baseball team | BUILDING 1685

Baseball was UGA's first varsity sport. A team formed in 1886 posted a 2-0 record, beating a town team from Athens and a team from Emory College, thanks to the ace pitching of Charles Ed Morris, who introduced the curve ball to the South. The team played on Herty Field on North Campus until moving in 1911 to Sanford Field on Central Campus, which it shared with the football team. After playing in several other locations, the team got a permanent home in 1966 at Foley Field. A $3.5 million renovation completed in 1990 created a complex considered one of the best in college baseball. With a capacity of 3,291, Foley Field features all chair-back seating; a partially covered grandstand with a concession area; indoor and outdoor bullpens and indoor hitting cages; spacious locker rooms; a players' lounge; coaches' offices; and exercise and training facilities. The stadium has hosted postseason events including SEC tournaments and NCAA regionals and super regionals.

The Diamond Dogs have played in the College World Series six times, winning the 1990 NCAA National Championship and reaching the championship game in 2008. The team has won six SEC titles, and seventeen

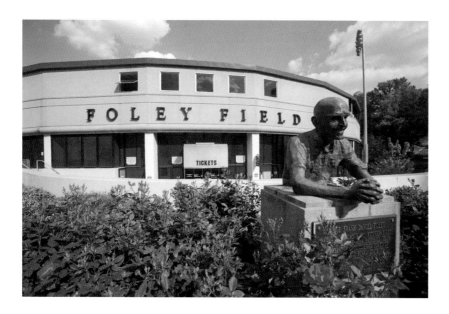

Dan Magill

Dan Magill is often called the greatest Bulldog of them all. The Athens native, who celebrated his ninety-second birthday in 2013, watched Georgia beat Yale in the first football game in Sanford Stadium in 1929 and has spent most of his life around UGA athletics. After lettering in tennis at UGA in 1940–41 and receiving a degree in journalism in 1942, he became the university's sports information director in 1949, holding the position until 1976. In 1954, he became head coach of the men's tennis team, which over the next thirty-four years compiled a 706–183 record, the best in NCAA Division I history when he stepped down. His teams won two national championships and thirteen SEC outdoor and eight SEC indoor titles. Five of his players won individual national titles, and fifteen were all-Americans. Magill was chiefly responsible for bringing more than twenty NCAA men's and women's tennis championships to Athens and for relocating the ITA Men's Collegiate Tennis Hall of Fame to UGA. He founded the Georgia Bulldog Club, started the *Georgia Bulldog* newspaper, and created several state and regional tennis tournaments. A former NCAA coach of the year, he has been inducted into the National Tennis Hall of Fame, the Southern Collegiate Tennis Hall of Fame, and the Georgia Sports Hall of Fame, and has received the prestigious J. D. Morgan Award. The press box in Sanford Stadium is named for Magill.

players have earned all-America honors a total of thirty-four times. Many players have been drafted into the majors, including eight first-round picks.

Frank Foley, from Columbus, Georgia, pitched for the 1908 Bulldog team, which won twenty straight games—a record that still stands—and captured UGA's first Southern Conference championship. After graduating, he earned a law degree at the University of Michigan and practiced law in Columbus, where he also served as judge of Recorder's Court. He was president of the State Bar of Georgia and served on the University System Board of Regents.

Dan Magill Tennis Complex

BUILT: 1977, with several additions | NAMED FOR: Dan Magill, former tennis coach and sports information director | CURRENT USE: UGA tennis program | BUILDINGS 2622, 2623, 1670, 1679

With sixteen courts and total seating capacity of more than five thousand, the Dan Magill Tennis Complex is one of the largest and finest on-campus tennis facilities in the country as well as home to one of the nation's top collegiate tennis programs. Named for a legend in collegiate tennis and one of UGA's most beloved figures, the Magill complex includes Henry Feild Stadium, with six state-of-the-art courts; the Lindsey Hopkins Indoor Courts, with four courts; the McWhorter practice courts, with six courts; the ITA Men's Collegiate Tennis Hall of Fame, honoring the nation's best male college tennis players and coaches since the 1880s; and several support facilities.

Tennis at UGA dates back to at least 1898, when tennis courts were on North Campus just inside the fence that separates the quad from Broad Street. In the 1930s, six red-clay courts were built in the Central Campus area near what is now the Psychology-Journalism Building. Six dirt courts were opened in 1958 on the current site, and in 1968 they were converted to hard surface. Henry Feild Stadium, built in 1977, is named for the Bulldogs' number 1 player from 1964 to 1966; he died in a car accident in 1968. The Lindsey Hopkins Indoor Courts, constructed in 1980, can seat twelve hundred in the bleachers and eight hundred more on the floor. The facility was funded by the Atlanta businessman Lindsey Hopkins Jr. in honor of his son, Lindsey Hopkins III, who was captain of the UGA tennis team in 1959

and a two-time state collegiate champion. The McWhorter practice courts are named for Bob McWhorter, a record-setting football and baseball player in the early twentieth century who was Georgia's first football all-American. The courts are located where McWhorter Hall, an athletic dorm, stood until it was demolished in 2005. The tennis hall of fame, built in 1980 with financial support from the singer Kenny Rogers and his wife, Marianne, a native of Athens, contains more than eight hundred photographs and murals featuring hall of famers and NCAA champions dating back to 1883, when the first national tennis tournament was held. Items on display include rackets used by players of different eras, including replicas of those used by the first U.S. Davis Cup players in 1900, and a tennis rulebook from 1879, the first in the country. Lights were added to the Magill complex in 1991 thanks to a gift from the actress Kim Basinger, an Athens native. The complex has hosted more than twenty NCAA tennis championship tournaments.

The Bulldog tennis program consistently ranks among the nation's best. The men's team has won six NCAA championships and more than thirty SEC titles. The women's team has captured two national titles, three USTA/ITA national team titles, and eight SEC championships. The combined programs have produced twelve NCAA individual champions and scores of all-Americans.

UGA swimmers and divers train and compete in Gabrielsen Natatorium in the Ramsey Center, one of the finest collegiate aquatic venues in the country. The facility, with seating for two thousand spectators, includes an Olympic-caliber fifty-meter competition pool, which holds 844,000 gallons of water and can be configured into short- and long-course layouts; a diving pool, which is sixteen to seventeen feet deep, holds 525,000 gallons of water, and has one-meter and three-meter springboards and five diving platforms ranging in height from one to ten meters; and an instructional and recreational pool, which holds 130,000 gallons of water and has eight swimming lanes. Gabrielsen Natatorium has hosted NCAA and SEC swimming and diving championship meets and was the site of the 1997 World Championship Team Trials in diving. Between November 1995 and January 2013, the women's swim team won eighty-two straight meets in Gabrielsen Natatorium, setting the UGA record for the longest home winning streak in any sport. The natatorium is named for B. W. (Bump) Gabrielsen, the head swimming coach from 1948 to 1966.

Ramsey Student Physical Activities Center

BUILT: 1995 | NAMED FOR: Bernard B. and Eugenia A. Ramsey, leading UGA benefactors | LOCATION: East Campus | CURRENT USE: Student recreational and athletic center; UGA swimming, diving, and volleyball teams | BUILDING 1690

Hailed as the best collegiate recreational facility in the country by *Sports Illustrated* when it opened, the Ramsey Center covers a footprint larger than Sanford Stadium. Except for parking decks, the 385,411-square-foot building is the largest single structure on UGA's campus. It sits atop three thousand concrete pilings that, if laid end to end, would stretch twenty-four miles. The 1.5 million gallons of water in the three swimming pools in the center's Gabrielsen Natatorium would fill a line of gallon jugs stretching 283 miles.

Administratively, the center falls under the university's Division of Student Affairs, and its main purpose is to provide students with opportunities for exercise, physical fitness, and recreational athletic competition. In addition to swimming pools, the center has five gymnasia for basketball, volleyball, badminton, and indoor soccer; a rock-climbing wall; ten racquetball courts; two international squash courts; a ten-thousand-square-foot strength and conditioning room; an eighth-mile track; three multipurpose rooms; and an outdoor resource center. Offices of the Department of Health Promotion and Behavior and the Department of Kinesiology are in the building, along with labs for research and teaching in human health and fitness. Most of the center's $40 million cost is being paid off by user fees, though the Athletic Association contributed $7.8 million for its construction.

Bernard Ramsey, a 1937 UGA graduate, was an executive with Merrill Lynch & Co. who, with his wife, Eugenia, donated some $44 million to UGA. The gifts mostly supported academic programs but included $2.5 million to endow the upkeep and operations of the Ramsey Center.

The Ramsey Center is the home of the men's and women's varsity swimming and diving teams and the women's volleyball team. The men's swimming and diving team—the last men's athletic team created at UGA—started in 1926 as a swimming program at the Athens YMCA. The women's program began in 1974 when the women's club swim team asked Martha Washington, a physical education teacher, and Liz Murphey, an associate athletic director, to form a team for intercollegiate competition. Under the guidance of Jack Bauerle, who became head coach of the women's team in 1979 and the men's in 1983, Bulldog swimmers, particularly women, have attained national prominence. The women won five national championships and claimed eleven SEC titles between 1997 and 2013. Three Georgia swimmers have won the NCAA's Woman

of the Year award as the nation's top female student-athlete, making UGA the only school in the country with more than one recipient. Twenty-seven men and women swimmers have received NCAA Post-Graduate Scholarships, and Bulldog swimmers have amassed more than seven hundred all-America honors. Numerous swimmers have won NCAA and SEC individual titles. More than two dozen Bulldog swimmers have competed in the Olympics for the United States or for other nations.

Bauerle, a 1975 UGA graduate who set three school records as cocaptain of the men's swim team, ranks third among active coaches, with more than four hundred victories. Named national women's coach of the year five times and SEC coach of the year thirteen times, he was head coach of the 2008 U.S. Olympic swimming and diving team and led the U.S. women's team at the 2005 world championships.

Women's volleyball began as a club sport, and the team played its first intercollegiate season in 1978. The volleyball team has appeared in eight NCAA tournaments, twice reaching the Sweet Sixteen, and captured the SEC championship in 1985 and 1986. Three players have received a total of nine all-America honors, and thirty-three players have earned a total of sixty-three all-SEC honors. The three-court volleyball arena in the Ramsey Center has retractable bleachers that can seat 1,925 fans for home matches. The facility includes a training room, a theater-style video and scouting room, locker rooms, and a players' lounge with a Wi-Fi bar and nutrition station.

UGA Golf Course

BUILT: 1968 | LOCATION: 2600 Riverbend Road | CURRENT USE: UGA men's and women's golf teams

Several male students formed the university's first golf team in 1924 and played under the leadership of elected team captains until the first coach was named in 1930. The women's team was started in 1967 when Liz Murphey was hired as a physical education teacher and golf coach. The teams play on a beautiful but challenging par-72 course proclaimed by *Golf Digest* magazine to be one of the fifty best public courses in the nation. Designed by the famed golf-course architect Robert Trent Jones, the layout includes 7,240 yards of lush Bermuda fairways, strategically placed bunkers, and lightning-fast bent-grass greens. Recent renovations made the greens larger and more undulating and added mounds and pot bunkers that help keep the ball in play and improve drainage but make it harder to reach the pins. Though challenging, the popular course hosts more than forty-five thousand rounds annually. In addition to the course itself, the golf complex includes a three-tier driving range, a large Bermuda chipping green, a bent-grass putting green, and three practice bunkers with a Bermuda green. The UGA course has been the site of NCAA national and regional championship tournaments and SEC championship tournaments for men and women. The Liz Murphey Collegiate Classic, started in 1973, is one of the longest-running intercollegiate competitions for women in any sport.

The men's golf team has played in more than thirty NCAA national championship tournaments, winning the national title in 1999 and 2005 and placing in the top ten another eighteen times. The men have captured twenty-eight SEC championships, more than any other school in the conference. Several players have won individual national and SEC championships, and dozens have received all-America and all-SEC honors. Five golfers have been named SEC player of the year. Chris Haack, the head coach since 1996, has been national coach of the year twice and SEC coach of the year four times.

The Bulldog women's golf team won the NCAA national championship in 2001 and has finished twenty times in the top ten. Individual golfers finished in the top twenty at NCAA tournaments a total of thirty-six times, and three women have won individual national titles. The women have captured eleven SEC team championships, including an unprecedented three straight from 1997 to 1999, and have won a conference-best total of nineteen SEC team and individual titles. Twenty-seven women have been named all-Americans a combined forty-five times, and eight have been SEC golfer of the year. Several women have played on the Curtis Cup team, and coaches Liz Murphey and Beans Kelly were each named national coach of the year.

Turner Family Sports Complex

BUILT: Soccer stadium, 1998; softball stadium, 2004 | NAMED FOR: Hoyt "Jack" Turner, an Athens businessman and supporter of UGA athletic programs | LOCATION: South Milledge Avenue | CURRENT USE: UGA soccer and softball teams

The women's soccer and softball teams, formed in 1994 and 1996, played on the Intramural Fields and at other locations until 1998, when a soccer stadium was opened. A softball stadium was added in 2004, and in 2006 the facilities were named the Turner Family Sports Complex. The soccer stadium, with a capacity of 1,750, has an electronic scoreboard with digital video and graphics display, along with a clubhouse with locker rooms, video and training equipment, a kitchen and catering area, and a players' lounge. The stadium has hosted preliminary rounds of NCAA tournaments and the Georgia Nike Invitational. The softball stadium has a capacity of fourteen hundred and includes video and training equipment, a players' lounge, a kitchen and catering area, a game room, and other facilities. NCAA regional and super regional tournaments have been played at the stadium.

Jack Turner lettered in baseball and basketball at UGA and earned a business degree in 1953. An executive in the financial services industry, Turner was chairman of the Athletic Scholarship Endowment Program, a trustee of the University of Georgia Foundation, and a board member of the UGA Athletic Association and the UGA Alumni Association. In addition to significant contributions to the soccer and softball programs, his family endowed scholarships in football, men's and women's basketball, gymnastics, and baseball.

Several soccer players have earned all-America and Academic All-America honors, and more than thirty-five have made all-SEC teams. The softball team has twice made the Women's College World Series Final Four, won two SEC championships, and played in ten NCAA regional and five NCAA super regional tournaments.

Equestrian Complex

BUILT: 1993 | LOCATED: Bishop, Georgia | CURRENT USE: home of UGA equestrian team

Formed in 2001 as UGA's twenty-first varsity intercollegiate sport, the equestrian program quickly attained national prominence through early competitive success and its leadership in moving the sport toward full recognition by the NCAA, which classifies equestrian competition as an "emerging" sport. For its first eight years, the team trained and held meets at the university's animal science arena on Milledge Avenue. In 2009, UGA acquired a farm, located about twelve miles south of campus, that in 1996 had been the training site for the U.S. Olympic Dressage Team. The 109-acre farm had excellent practice equipment and boarding accommodations for horses, and is being further developed to meet the specific needs of equestrian competition. In its first eight years, the Bulldog equestrian team won five national championships, barely missing a sixth in 2011. The team has won six Southern Equestrian titles, including five consecutive titles from 2005 to 2009. The team lost just one dual meet at home in the first five years after the format was introduced. Four riders have won individual national championships, and when the first-ever all-America teams in varsity equestrian were chosen in 2011, eight UGA riders won a total of ten honors.

SOURCES

The information in this book was compiled from contemporary publications and many websites, not from primary sources or original research. The following list of sources includes those I consulted most often. I also drew information from two academic papers written by students, from many pamphlets and brochures, and from dozens of newspaper and magazine articles. I relied on writers of varying skill and experience, and their facts and accounts did not always agree. More than once I ran into contradictions or discrepancies in the date of an event, or in descriptions and narratives of events and the people involved in them. Differing dates were particularly common for buildings, mainly because some sources dated a building from when construction started, some from when construction ended, and some from when additions or renovations were completed. In cases of conflicting information, I generally used the information commonly agreed on by the most sources. Because this is not a scholarly book, and because I wanted it to be accessible, I intentionally avoided formal citations such as footnotes or endnotes, but everything in the book can be documented in one or more of the sources I used.

Boney, F. N. *A Pictorial History of the University of Georgia*. 2nd ed. Athens: University of Georgia Press, 2000.

———. *A Walking Tour of the University of Georgia*. Athens: University of Georgia Press, 1989.

Bowen, Joel Thomas. "Room To Grow: A Historical Analysis of the Physical Growth at the University of Georgia 1785 to 1990." PhD dissertation, University of Georgia, 1990.

Brooks, Robert Preston. *The University of Georgia under Sixteen Administrations, 1785–1955*. Athens: University of Georgia Press, 1956.

Coleman, Kenneth, ed. *A History of Georgia*. 2nd ed. Athens: University of Georgia Press, 1991.

Coulter, E. Merton. *College Life in the Old South*. Athens: University of Georgia Press, 1951.

Dooley, Vince. *History and Reminiscences of the University of Georgia*. Decatur, Ga.: Looking Glass Books, 2011.

Doster, Emily Jean, and Gary L. Doster. *Postcard History Series, Athens*. Charleston, S.C.: Arcadia Publishing, 2011.

Dyer, Thomas G. *The University of Georgia: A Bicentennial History, 1785–1985*. Athens: University of Georgia Press, 1985.

Goodman, Hugh. "The South Campus of the University of Georgia: An Architectural History, 1906–1941." *Atlanta History* 35, no. 1 (Spring 1991): 5–24.

Hester, Conoly, and Albert L. Hester. *Athens, Georgia: Celebrating 200 Years at the Millennium*. Montgomery, Ala.: Community Communications, 1999.

Hynds, Ernest. *Antebellum Athens and Clarke County Georgia*. Athens: University of Georgia Press, 1974.

Izlar, Bob. *The Centennial History of Forestry in Georgia: A Pictorial Journey*. Virginia Beach, Va.: Donning Company, 2006.

Jerrolds, Bob W. *The History of the College of Education, the University of Georgia*. Athens: University of Georgia College of Education, 1989.

Magill, Dan. *Dan Magill's Bull-Doggerel: Fifty Years of Anecdotes from the Greatest Bulldog Ever*. Atlanta: Longstreet Press, 1993.

Mize, Jessie J. *The History of Home Economics at the University of Georgia*. Athens, Ga.: Agee Publishers, 1983.

Murray, Calvin Clyde, Paul Tabor, R. H. Driftmier, Frederick William Bennett, and George Harris King. *History of the College of Agriculture of the University of Georgia*. Athens, Ga.: Agricultural Alumni Association, 1975.

Sniff, Daniel. F. "The Space Between: A Developmental History of Open Space, Lawns and Gardens of the American Campus and a History of Herty Field." Master's thesis, University of Georgia, 2011.

———. "The Sustainable Movement and the Future Effect on Campus Development for the University of Georgia." Master's thesis, University of Georgia, 2008.

Thomas, Frances Taliaferro. *A Portrait of Historic Athens and Clarke County*. 2nd ed. Athens: University of Georgia Press, 2009.

2011 Georgia Football Media Guide. Athens: UGA Sports Communications Office, 2011.

Wood, Gwen Y. *A Unique and Fortuitous Combination: An Administrative History of the University of Georgia School of Law*. Athens: University of Georgia Law School Association, 1998.

IMAGE CREDITS

Greg Gotsch, office of the University Architects for Facilities Planning,
University of Georgia: 23, 69, 89, 129, 145, 169

Hargrett Rare Book and Manuscript Library, The University of Georgia
Libraries: viii (Georgia Photo Files, MS3705, box 11, folder 71), xviii, 5
(Georgia Photo Files, MS3705, box 12, folder 47), 6 (Georgia Photo Files,
MS3705, Oversize University Pictures, Ag Hill Folder), 7 top (Georgia Photo
Files, MS3705, box 4, folder 108), 7 bottom (Georgia Photo Files, MS3705, box
12, folder 1), 10 (Official U.S. Navy Photograph, Georgia Photo Files, MS3705,
box 14, folder 36), 12 (University Print File, UA 97-113, box 2, folder 111), 22
(Georgia Photo Files, MS3705, box 11, folder 66), 25 top right (University
of Georgia Photo Album, MS 802), 25 bottom right (University of Georgia
Photo Album, MS 802), 28 (Georgia Photo Files, MS3705, box 11, folder 71), 93
(Wallace Richter Photographs, 1941–1943, UA 07-005, image 331), 134 (School
of Music, Hugh Hodgson Materials, UA 09-021, box 1), 135 bottom (Georgia
Photo Files, MS3705, box 4, folder 138), 148, 168 (Georgia Photo Files, MS3705,
box 11, folder 3), 170 (Georgia Photo Files, MS3705, box 15, folder 8), 184
(Georgia Photo Files, MS3705, box 7, folder 80)

University of Georgia Photographic Services

Tori Bauer: 94 (19221-s006)

Paul Efland: 13 (27624-077), 24 (25743-014), 25 left (22230-019), 26 (26773-037),
34 (26902-051), 48 (29015-117), 49 (21338-021), 57 (26897-011), 61 (25688-005), 64
(29017-032), 66 (26123-021), 70 (23775-014), 74 (25846-019), 75 (25820-003), 92
(24496-027), 96 (23785-031), 99 (25994-016), 100 (19792-024), 102 (24467-031),
105 (24702-030), 109 (24135-014), 113 (22971-011), 120 (27810-004), 122 (20764-
040), 126 (25833-010), 132 (22048-011), 142 (25751-016), 158 (27748-017), 161
(25752-087), 175 (27803-020), 179 (27334-027)

Nancy Evelyn: 39 (22893-075), 54 (20543-010), 81 (21526-009), 84 (20884-072), 130 (21034-026), 131 (21031-004)

Peter Frey: 27 (24592-005), 30 (26752-020), 36 (17441-s002), 38 (24793-075), 58 (25552-005), 59 (20887-002), 73 (29028-025), 76 (26446-027), 91 (28857-021), 133 (27141-003), 135 top (25076-045), 140 (27663-106), 153 (27635-031), 156 (25426-098), 160 (20520-021), 176 (20898-063)

Dorothy Kozlowski: 111 (25835-002), 149 (28722-004)

Robert Newcomb: 50 (28635-006), 141 (21820-004), 166 (27635-031), 183 (26764-008),

Beth Newman: 60 (24704-024), 79 (24705-027), 106 (23576-003), 116 (24706-010), 124 (23724-005), 155 top (23575-003), 155 bottom (23575-007)

Rick O'Quinn: 15 (14884-04-n027), 20 (25162-002), 43 bottom (19844-003), 119 (25021-018), 121 (19935-004), 171 (21967-014)

Dot Paul: ii (28146-053), vi (25239-077), xii (28447-014), 37 (28352-256), 40 top (28430-006), 40 bottom (28433-013), 45 (25842-032), 63 (29750-030), 72 (26326-036), 77 (22981-001), 95 (26696-006), 98 (26693-009), 101 (21287-003), 104 (29000-007), 107 (23124-004), 110 (22984-011), 112 (22974-027), 114 (24393-011), 123 (26690-002), 136 (20809-024), 137 (25936-103), 138 (25613-007), 162 (29001-083), 163 (29266-093), 173 (29240-222), 181 (25242-018), 187 (21741-055)

Andrew Davis Tucker: 29 (25194-021), 31 (28645-030), 33 (26708-020), 43 top (25792-155), 46 (24564-014), 47 (26199-004), 52 (25193-014), 65 (26333-021), 103 (26226-002), 146 (25767-061), 151 (25965-001), 165 (26043-023), 178 (27057-018), 185 (26883-014)

INDEX

for, 133; in Demosthenian Literary Society, 27; on gymnastics team, 95, 124, 168, 179–82, 189; sororities for, 58, 93, 122; in sports, 167, 177, 181, 186–90; in teacher training, 43–44, 92; Title IX legislation and, 168, 187

Woodruff, George "Kid," 177

Woodruff Hall, 67, 76, 180

Woodruff Practice Fields, 125, 177

World War I, 8, 71, 78

World War II, 10, 87, 150

Wray, Thomas, 146

Wray-Nicholson House, 143, 146–47

Wright, J. B., Jr., 133

WUGA (radio), 119

WUGA-TV, 76

yearbook (*Pandora*), 5, 51, 70

YMCA, 78, 180

Yoculan, Suzanne, 181–82

Zell B. Miller Learning Center, 18, 68, 72–73

Zoology Department, 94

This book is set in ITC Legacy Serif and Legacy Sans.
Ronald Arnholm, professor of art at the University of Georgia,
Lamar Dodd School of Art, designed the Legacy font family
for the International Typeface Corporation. Legacy Roman
is based on the typeface cut by Nicolas Jenson in Venice,
1470; Legacy Italic is based on an italic typeface by
Claude Garamond, 1566.